ROOMS

Create the home you want for your life

ROOMS

Create the home you want for your life

DECLAN O'DONNELL

HACHETTE
BOOKS
IRELAND

Copyright © 2016 text, Declan O'Donnell

First published in 2016 by Hachette Books Ireland
An Hachette UK Company

1

A CIP catalogue record for this title is available from the British Library.

ISBN 978 1473 628335

Typeset in Akzidenz Grotesk by Anú Design, Tara
Cover and text design by Anú Design, Tara
Printed in Germany by Mohn Media

Cover images: ODKM Architects and Ned Kelly/Imageart Photography (far left);
ODKM Architects and Infinity Media (centre left); Dulux Paints Ireland (centre right and far right)

Hachette Books Ireland policy is to use papers that are natural, renewable and recyclable products
and made from wood grown in sustainable forests. The logging and manufacturing processes are
expected to conform to the environmental regulations of the country of origin.

Hachette Books Ireland
8 Castlecourt Centre
Castleknock
Dublin 15
Ireland

A division of Hachette UK, Carmelite House, 50 Victoria Embankment, London EC4Y 0DZ, England
www.hachettebooksireland.ie

To my parents John and Maggie –

for every home they made for Orlaith, Ciaran, Aine and myself –

and for the sacrifices they made to always put us first.

And in memory of my gran, Jean Corrigan, who showed all of us

what making a home is all about.

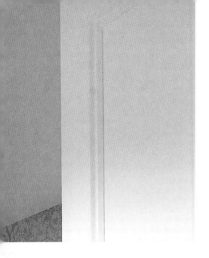

contents

introduction

My name is Declan O'Donnell, and I am an architect. I am passionate about architecture and design and have been working in the industry for almost twelve years, although my journey began back in 1998 with my undergraduate degree in architecture at Queen's University in Belfast. It takes seven to ten years to qualify as an architect, and it's not easy, so you have to have real passion for it, but when you get bitten by it, it's hard to go back. People say it's a vocation, and they're at least half-right. It has changed my life.

It took me a while to really get what architecture is. It's more than drawings and designing, it's a lifestyle, a way of thinking, and a way of approaching problem-solving. At its best, it's more than the sum of its parts. It has to be practical and functional, but it also has great scope to connect with your spirit, and it can move you.

After finishing at Queen's, I worked in Dublin for a year and then moved to Glasgow to study for a postgraduate diploma and this is when things really kicked off for me.

I was studying within the grounds of a spectacular piece of architecture, the Glasgow School of Art, a seminal building designed by Charles Rennie Mackintosh. It was a truly inspirational place to study and, as soon as I landed in Glasgow, I knew that becoming an architect was what I wanted to achieve. When I finished my diploma, I was invited to join one of the largest and most prestigious architecture firms in the world – Foster and Partners in London. I jumped at it, and worked there for almost five years during which time I learned everything about how to design and manage projects of differing scales, all across the globe. A lot of what I know today I owe to the time I spent there, and I am forever grateful for that opportunity.

However, in time, I decided I wanted to do my own thing. I was working on huge projects in Vietnam, New York and London, and I felt disconnected from the more human side of what architecture can offer. In 2009, I decided to come back to Dublin to set up ODKM Architects with two former colleagues … in a shop window … in the midst of a fairly deep recession! Not great timing but, funnily enough, not bad timing either. I am a natural optimist, something that definitely helped.

I think the recent recession in Ireland has been the best thing to happen to Irish design in the past twenty years because it has put design back at the centre of what it is all about – to live in places and to be present – and that's really important. Real design isn't about squandering vast amounts of money, it's about the subtlety of light, materials, details and texture and, after that, innovation. It is to create perfect spaces suited to their environments and to the needs of the people who use them. That's what I came back to Dublin for. Architecture brings people together, and that's what I enjoy most about practising today.

I want to do just one thing with this book: I want anyone who reads it to embrace the power of design and make a change for the better in how they live. Ultimately – and this is what good design is all about; it should make a positive impact in your everyday life, both from a practical point of view, but also from an emotive one – you should feel happier if you have good design going on around you. This book aims to show you what that looks and feels like, to get the creative juices going, and also help bridge that gap between being inspired, and making practical moves to improve your home. Rest assured, it is easier than you think.

I want to debunk the whole mystery about what design is. There is no doubt design can be daunting and, dare I say it, almost elitist. I understand why this puts people off but it really frustrates me. Architecture and design are all about self-expression, figuring out spaces and making homes work for whoever lives in them. It's about happiness, comfort, peace and fun. I don't care what your budget is, what stage in life you are at, whether you live in a tiny apartment or a lake house. None of that matters. All that matters is finding out who you are and how you want to live, so that you can be happier in your home. That's the ultimate goal, no matter what the magazines tell you. This book keeps it simple and will help you to think about how you live in your home.

Design is not only a tool to create a truly unique home, it also enables us to completely rethink *how* we live. When we do this right, it can really improve the quality of our lives. I know it sounds a bit over the top, but it's true.

You may feel like you need more space but are trying to decide between an attic conversion and an extension. You might simply want to add some extra space or revamp a well-worn home. Whatever you want to do, my aim in writing this book is to show you how any space can be improved with a little thinking and good design.

In the following chapters, we'll look at how you can use the space that you have in a completely different way to change the way you live for the better. We'll also look at the dos and don'ts, and the ups and downs of extensions and how to really make these work for you.

I strongly believe that good design and architecture are for everyone. The environment around you, be it your living room, your kitchen or your favourite restaurant, they all have qualities that directly influence your mood, and there are reasons you like them. We are connected to our surroundings, and we feed off them. They speak to us.

People change and move homes for lots of different reasons, and it's usually related to what stage they are at in life. From first-time buyers to those looking to downsize, growing families to unexpected career moves, nowadays instead of just moving house and trading up, more and more people are being more creative with the spaces they have and there's a real move to improve and update the houses in which we already live. Economic forces are always at play as well – sometimes it makes more sense to improve what you have already instead of selling up and moving.

Most of us like the area we live in. The kids are in school, friends live nearby and there is a familiarity there that is comforting. There's a lot to be said for refurbishing a house rather than moving – and it's a great opportunity to get stuck in and create the home you've always wanted.

While the glorious, restful *feeling* of getting home after a long day exists no matter what, I have been in hundreds of houses over the years and the harsh reality is that I see simple layout problems or space issues that can be solved easily with a bit of clever thinking – and trust me, it's the small things that make the biggest difference. I've seen hillwalkers with nowhere for their rain gear, avid golfers with a hallway full of golf clubs, and families with truckloads of toys cluttering their only family space. You name it, I've seen it. I think we slide into these bad habits over time, and with time comes a certain obliviousness followed by an unknowing acceptance of a new norm.

Good design can solve almost any problem in a house and can bring life to even the most lived-in homes. All that personality and individuality that we all possess shouldn't be buried so deep, lying undiscovered, repressed and dormant. It should scream from the rooftops, stamp all over the place you call home and bring joy to you and those you invite through the door. That's living.

I love figuring out how spaces work, how to make something better, bigger, brighter or more comfortable. This will directly determine the feeling you will have in a new space. Maybe decluttering the utility room by designing a new multi-level storage unit will hit the nail on the head and solve that problem, but the success of this will be measured by how you feel about it when it's finished. Do you feel more calm when you're in there? Do you feel less stressed when trying to find something? Do you spend less time in there now because it is ordered? Is it easier now? Are you a bit happier dealing with the lorryloads of washing because it's more organised? If the answer is yes, then this is the determining factor of how we evaluate good design – how it makes us feel. That's it. Simple!

As you read this book, I want you to get excited by the opportunities that are out there. You may think of them as problems, but really they are opportunities to come up with a solution that works for you. Everything you do, every day, can be improved through design. So whatever it is that isn't working for you, grab hold of it and fix it. Big or small, don't keep living with the same issues that you know are driving you mad!

In this book, I've put together helpful design tips that we use over and over again, because they have been proven to work and pretty much every client I speak to has these same issues. I want you to gain some of that inner designer spirit, and tackle the problems (sorry, opportunities) that your home presents. It doesn't matter about the size of your home, or your budget, there is always an answer.

My advice in this book is to get stuck in and give it a go. Understanding the problem is the first port of call for any design challenge, so you really need to get to the bottom of the issues at hand, as well as figure out who you are and what makes you tick.

The essence of this is to acknowledge what makes you really happy, because if you can nail that then you will have something special.

The advice in this book covers renovations, extensions and new builds, but a lot of it is focussed on what you already have in terms of space – it's not about self-builds (that's a book in itself!). Instead, it's about exploring the design principles that should be at the core of extending or renovating your home, and how to make it work for you. As well as this, it's about getting inspired and looking at how other people have tackled similar problems and embraced clever design thinking to achieve great results.

Let's start.

where
to start

I think a lot of people don't know where to start when they are looking to renovate or change their living space, and this calls a halt to their greatest plans before they ever get going. Cluttered hallways, boring bathrooms or that room that just doesn't know exactly what it is supposed to be — people end up living their lives surrounded by unanswered design issues.

Spaces that don't work drive us all mad, and yet they endure. Changing them can seem so daunting and unmanageable at the beginning, but the key is not where to start, but how to start.

Architecture and good design are for everyone. We are all designers in our own right because, at its very essence, designing is about comfort. Carrying this thought through to the everyday can really unlock a whole new way of living.

There are simple tools to achieve this transformation and they revolve around simplicity. Always understand the space you are dealing with. This might mean measuring it out and doing a scaled drawing (or getting someone to do one for you). We all understand space, even if we think we don't. If you have a small sitting room, think about how much furniture should go in there, and what size it should be. Two big chairs might be better than a sofa — radical as that may sound — but it might be the key to making a smaller room work.

> "Function has to come before everything else and it will offer up rules that shouldn't be broken in terms of flow, space, light and usability."

What I'm talking about here is function. Function has to come before everything else and it will offer up rules that shouldn't be broken in terms of flow, space, light and usability. Even the most creative designer can't change the physical space that they are working with, but what we can certainly do is react to it — and that's the key. When you get the function right, you can start to have more fun with it and push things around a little, but if it is wrong it doesn't matter what you do with it — it will still be wrong, and you will *feel* it because it won't work.

There are some rules that you should swear by, and others you should break. I always challenge people to think about the conventional notion of what a door is or what a window is or whether any doors are needed between rooms at all, even into hallways. The rules say we need them, but these rules can be bent and broken in the right circumstances, if it makes sense to do so. Common conventions *should* be challenged. Architects do this all the time, through big ideas and small, but it all adds up. Good design is responsive, which means it reacts to something, and as it starts with you, there is no reason for you not to embrace it and put it at the very centre of your home and your life.

I generally think we need to get back to what is important, to live more slowly and really think about who and what is important to us in our homes, and then put these things at the centre of our home-making. Strip away the nonsense that doesn't

resonate with you, decide what it is that you cannot live without and surround yourself with those things. No fillers. We don't need more space, we need more design and more comfort to make the space we have work better for us.

THE DESIGN BRIEF

Good design does not start with drawing or sketching. It doesn't start with a selection of ideas or research images or a whole scrapbook of magazine cutouts. Whether you are designing a skyscraper or a cup holder, the process is remarkably similar (to a degree!). It all starts with you, and a whole lot of questions. The more questions you ask, the more successful your design will be and, eventually, you will distil the real essence of what you are trying to do. This questioning strips away all the fluff and gets to the core of the task at hand. When you reach this point, you are ready to begin. Whatever the project, big or small, they all start from this same place – your design brief.

The reason a design brief is so important is that there are countless design solutions for any given problem. You, however, are not looking for countless answers, you are looking for the specific answer to your specific needs at a particular moment in time.

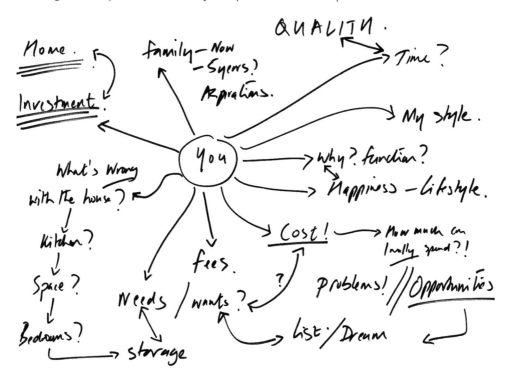

You'll hear designers talk endlessly about the design brief, and for good reason. A good brief puts all the relevant information and constraints of a project into one concise document, and it should clearly outline your take on the following:

Time:
How much time can you afford to spend on the project? Time in meetings, time making decisions and talking through options, time spent deciding on finishes, attending site meetings, fighting with your architect ;) – and, of course, time out of the house if you are refurbishing extensively.

Cost:
What can you realistically afford to spend? Kitchen, lighting, flooring, bathrooms, landscaping, windows, insulation, plumbing, professional fees, etc., it all adds up, so create a spreadsheet and make a long list.

As a general rule, I always advise anyone to pick two from cost, quality and time and allow the other to be sacrificed, as you can't have all three – so it's really worthwhile thinking about this. Most people want the best quality they can afford, and that's what you should aim for.

As a general rule, you can only have 2!!

Quality:
This is a great question to think about, what kind of quality are you aiming for? Top? Mid? Low? This will impact on both cost and time, as there's no such thing as getting the absolute best work quickly and at a cheap rate.

Disruption:
How much disruption can you handle?

Rooms:
What rooms do you need? What space issues do you have?

Function:
How do you live? What's not working? What is working? What does the fix look like? Think about how you live, what you enjoy and what makes you happy. What is the routine of the house? How should it be adapted? What are you demanding from your home?

Sustainability:
Energy efficiency is better for the environment and it can save you money, but it can also add extra costs upfront so, how important is this to you?

Style:
You don't have to know your style fully yet, it will come, but if you have a strong design style then show it!

Design: ODKM Architects; Image: Declan O'Donnell

The design brief is such an important document because it will force you to think clearly about your budget, your ideas, the positives in your existing house, and what doesn't work for you. It will outline your needs, wants, timeframes, budget, problems, disruption, style, feeling and everything else you can think of. When you establish your brief, it will be the framework for your entire project.

Whether you are working with an architect or just thinking about renovating your home, putting your design brief together is crucial. This is why I get frustrated when someone comes to me stating that they already know what they want or that they want something that has been done before for someone else. Designing doesn't work like that, it has to be tailored, and good design comes from reacting to a space and creating a good design brief.

You can't really know what you want until you go through this process and establish your brief. The design brief will reveal your real wants and needs, because you will be challenged during the initial design stage, and your needs may become more apparent. Having preconceived ideas of what you want before you do the brief can be a bad idea as when you start thinking about budget and practical issues, plans can and do change.

1. Why do you want to renovate your current home?

2. What is your lifestyle? Do you spend a lot of time at home? Do you work at home? Do you entertain often?

3. How much time do you spend in each of the areas: living room, bedroom, kitchen, utility space, etc?

4. What kind of spaces do you think you need (e.g. bedrooms, bigger kitchen, family room, bathrooms)?

5. What do you think the renovation should look like?

6. What do you think your present home lacks?

7. How much can you realistically afford in terms of cost, time and quality?

8. How soon would you like to be settled into your redesigned home? Are there rigid time constraints?

9. Do you have strong ideas about design? What are your design preferences?

10. What qualities are you looking for in an architect?

11. Is there anyone in the family with a disability? Do you envisage staying in the house for a number of years? Mobility problems brought on by ageing may need to be addressed.

12. Do you want to pursue options, and establish the additional inputs required, to achieve zero energy outcomes, using healthy materials? Do you have any other sustainability goal?

Until you have everything laid out in the design brief, you can't start addressing the problems and figuring out the right solutions for you.

An open mind is the best design tool you can have.

When we start a project, we always send out a list of around twenty questions to help our clients start developing their design brief. Most of these are very practical (Describe your current home … What do you like about it? What's missing? What don't you like? Do you want to change the space you have?) and enable us to get a clear idea of the client and their home. Left are some of the more pertinent questions that everyone should think about at the very beginning of their project.

I always enjoy talking through the answers to these questions because what I am really interested in is lifestyle. Who cooks? Who gets up early? Who works from home? Who plays sports, and what sports do they play? When is the busiest time in the house? The more we (and you) know about the day-to-day running of your house, then the better equipped you will be to make it work for you.

I remember a project for a family who were all avid golfers. They kept saying this to me and I hadn't really appreciated it until I visited the house. In the hallway, I found endless golf bags (and a few trolleys). It wasn't a small hallway (thankfully) but it was a bit crazy. It's an example of how something that is part of your everyday lifestyle needs to be designed for – because if you don't, you will spend a lifetime tripping over golf clubs.

We'll now look at the main elements of a design brief.

Budget

A fundamental part of your design brief is, of course, your budget. Every project has one. The key is not to let it constrict you.

You can still aim high – good design isn't about money, it's about ideas.

The first thing you need to do is to put a spreadsheet together, and include on it every item that will be involved in your renovation. This will give you the overall financial picture. It will be a long list: fixtures and fittings, contingency fund, professional fees, kitchen, flooring, bathrooms, finishes, landscaping, decorating, built-in furniture, lighting, furnishings, plumbing, electrical works, heating upgrades, insulation, roof works, garden walls, electric gates, fuse boards, electricity meter boxes … the list goes on and on.

"Be realistic about how much you can afford, and stick to it."

Be realistic about how much you can afford, and stick to it. In an ideal world, your budget would cover everything on your wish list. In truth, this is seldom possible, and again illustrates why it's so important to get the design brief right – so you know what it is you want and how you want to achieve it.

At some point you may have to start prioritising from the brief, so a good clear understanding of what you want and what you need is important.

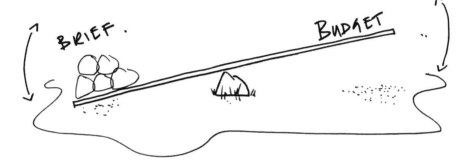

You $ Architect =

Design process begins....

.... Hold on, I should probably mention something about BUDGET here ...

Don't forget to include professional fees and a contingency for building work. Despite mountains of detailed drawings, there is no getting away from the fact that building is clunky, and there is usually a change or two along the way, so you need to factor in around 5–10 per cent of the total budget for this contingency cost.

Value versus cost

This is something I talk to all my clients about. The reason is that there are always different levels of value attributed to different costs. For example, in a small kitchen renovation with a limited budget, I would put more value on installing large glass sliding doors than I would on very expensive cabinets. The reason is that without the large glass sliding doors, the room and the space will suffer terribly. These items may be so integral to the whole design that, without them, you could question whether to do the job in the first place. For this reason, the value of the glass sliding doors far outweighs their cost, and you will still be able to install a really cool (albeit not quite so expensive) kitchen.

Design: ODKM Architects; Image: Sasfi Hope Ross

Ergonomics

This is the science behind how we as humans interact with the objects and the world around us. Ergonomics should inform everything you design. It's about comfortably negotiating spaces, and using space in a controlled and simple way. You don't notice it when it's done correctly because it is effortless. But when the ergonomics are wrong, it can be a train wreck. Dining tables usually cause the most problems ergonomically. People are forever trying to squeeze in a table that won't fit or that you can't successfully walk around if someone is sitting in a chair. How many times have you had to clumsily trip over behind someone sitting at a dining table to get out? This is bad ergonomics, and it drives me crazy. You should work out how much space you need between things for them to be used comfortably.

Seating

We are comfortable with our bottoms 450 mm off the finished floor level – this is the height of most standard office or dining chairs. More comfortable seating, such as loungers or sofas, are closer to 350–400 mm, but this is for lounging only. A good bench seat needs to be 450 mm high and around 450 mm deep for optimum comfort.

Tables

A desk to work at is usually 750 mm high, or a bit less if it's a more informal table. As a rule, I would never drop below 700 mm as this will start to impact the athletes sitting down who might have muscular thighs, as they will struggle to get their knees under the table! This is an absolute no-no. Universal comfort is what we're aiming for here, and that's what ergonomics is all about.

Context

In design, as in life, context is king. This means understanding the problem you face and getting to grips with its constraints. Every project has constraints (size, budget, location, timeframes, etc.) and I think we shy away from things we don't want to deal with – we kind of avoid them and pretend that they don't exist – but we really have to face them head-on to start to understand them. This is essential if you are actually going to fix the problem at hand. If you do not fully understand your design challenge and what you want to achieve – in all its complexity and under the endless criteria that it must abide by – then you might as well scribble rockets flying to the moon.

When you put the brief together with your budget, and have examined and analysed your current setup and questioned everything, only then will you have a grasp of the context. This is essential in order to ensure that you start down the right road. In any given context, any amount of design decisions can work – but you have to start by understanding the context you are working in.

Orientation

The orientation of a building is the first thing I look at when visiting a property. Where the sun comes up in the morning and where it sets at night are fundamental factors that can dictate what happens in each room, or how it is decorated, which may depend on the amount of natural light it gets. There is nothing worse than missing the sun all day long or feeling like you're always on the wrong side of the house.

East-facing rooms are perfect for kitchens as they catch the warmth and brightness of the morning sun. The evening sun is generally welcomed in living areas, where the warm glow of sunshine can penetrate deep into the room to keep it warm and welcoming. This is not only important for the comfort levels in the house, but environmentally as well. A passive solar strategy is something you should be aware of because it will ensure both comfort and performance is optimised, and will help to reduce your heating bills.

As a general rule, open up a house in such a way that living spaces and open areas are embracing the south-facing sun. To the north, keep the window openings smaller, and arrange the more ancillary spaces, such as storage/utility, here. If you can get a ray of sunshine through your bedroom window first thing in the morning, you won't regret it, so try and get these facing east if you can.

I remember a client who came to me to 'rearrange' her house. She had the most magnificent back garden, huge mature trees at the back and a luscious verdant lawn with beautifully layered shrubbery along the sides. The only problem was that the rear of the house faced north, and so the rooms that looked out over this garden were dark most of the time because they never got any direct sunlight. Now, you can't re-orientate a house, but you can try. We extended the back wall of the house into the garden to a point where we could capture the south-facing sunlight as it crept over the main ridge of the house through a huge skylight. It wasn't a lot, but it was something. This, combined with opening up the spaces at the back, meant the garden could now be enjoyed fully all year round, and the space was much brighter and airier as a result. Know your orientation – it's important.

"Know your orientation – it's important."

Layout

The famous French architect Le Corbusier coined the phrase that homes are 'machines for living', so before you spend all your money on a flash paint job, make sure the engine is working properly. When I talk about the engine, I mean the layout.

Layout is everything. This is something that you actually can get 'wrong', so it is worth putting serious time, effort and thought into it. Teasing out the layout comes by evaluating every item on the design brief simultaneously. Think of it as a mathematical equation – it's that logical.

Design: ODKM Architects; Image: Barbara Egan

In a small room, look at how it is accessed and how this affects the room. Sometimes just changing the swing of an internal door – or, indeed, changing a swing door to a sliding door or removing the door altogether – can completely change how the room opens up, and therefore how it can be used. Think about rooms and how you want them to feel, as well as how you will use them. Is the living room big enough? Where does the television go? Is the dining room part of the kitchen or separate from it?

This is also a very practical exercise. Think about what rooms should be beside each other; the kitchen beside the utility room, the living room opening to the hallway, connected to the kitchen, etc. You should be brave, because sometimes being brave is also being clever, and is often exactly the right thing to do.

A great example I always love to see is an upside-down house. They're called upside-down houses because the owners have flipped the layout to put the living rooms and kitchen upstairs, and the bedrooms downstairs. This is usually done to get more sun into the living areas, or to avail of a nice view (the context). Clever thinking, making big changes in how we live. I love all that.

If you are significantly rearranging the spaces in your home, you really need to make sure that the layout is right for you in the long term. If you are trying to create *new* spaces within your home, look at the layout of an existing room and ask yourself the following two questions: What is it about the current layout that is *not* working? What will the main function of this room be?

We are all different, we all live differently and different things make different people happy. This is why the design brief is so fundamental to a good project, because it is unique to you, and to really understand this is to make a better home for you.

Fabric first

When working through the design brief, it can be tricky to figure out what is important or what should take priority. There will be compromise, and you will be challenged, which means your initial ideas may change – they may have to.

Ultimately, it's about prioritising what is important, and I would always recommend that you concentrate on the big-ticket items that you will only do once. You'll quickly have a million things to think about, so it is easy to become distracted and take your eye off something that is really more important than something else.

We have a saying in the office, 'fabric first' – this relates to the fabric of the building: the walls, floors, windows, ceilings and roofs. It's an obvious place to start, but, generally speaking, you will only do these things once, so it's really vital to do them right, otherwise you may find yourself having to revisit them again in a few years' time.

There is no point installing an expensive hardwood floor if you haven't insulated underneath it, for example. We say this because, in managing a large project, you need to look at the big picture and think long-term about your goals. Is this your home for life? Is it a home for five to ten years? Will you definitely be moving at some stage? The answers to these questions will drastically change the design of a project. A building is like an old bike, you need to look after it and maintain it so that you can freewheel down the hills and enjoy it without the back wheel coming off.

Finishes

When you have thought about your style and the overall feeling you want to achieve, you'll need to make some decisions on the materials you need, including flooring, wall decor, windows, lighting, fixtures and furnishings. These are the elements that not only make your home look good, they are also what will evoke a feeling or a sense of style. These are the things that bring a home to life.

The design process for choosing these elements is the same. Start with logic. Practicality is key here, so think about each room. What is going to happen here? What material properties will complement what happens? For example, in a kitchen, the emphasis could be on durability and ease of maintenance – something hard-wearing, practical yet beautiful, and something that can take the occasional spill without you having to worry about damage. Living rooms may want something much more soft and cosy, so the flooring and furnishings should reflect that.

This is all about making informed decisions, and this comes back to the design brief and the research you carried out through that process.

Function

Form follows function – this is the design mantra of the many and if there's one rule to follow (and not break) it is this one.

Before style, colour, furniture or anything else, function is the absolute starting point for every decision you will make in designing your home. If it doesn't function, then it's just style over substance. When it comes to your home – which, after all, is among anyone's biggest investments – if something doesn't do the job it is intended to do, then it is not only bad design, but a very expensive mistake.

Subjective versus objective

The decision-making involved in choosing the finishes and materials to kit out a room or a house can be daunting. Where do I start? How can I tell what is right or what will work?

The answer to the first question – Where do I start? – is completely objective. Forget the emotional side of the brain for a second and weigh up your options. Remove yourself from what you do or don't 'like'. Ask yourself hard questions that will only have a limited number of answers. In the area you are changing, does it suit hard or soft flooring? Should it be light or dark? Should it be natural or man-made?

When you have answered these questions, you are ready to start whittling down your options. This is an important cognitive step to take because, in design, it is these answers that can be 'wrong' for the task at hand, so you have to make sure you get them right.

When you have done this, answering the second question – How can I tell what will work? – becomes much more fun. This is all about your own subjectivity – or put another way, it is what you actually like. This is a fun stage because nobody (me included) can tell you what you like. If you like a jungle-themed wallpaper, it doesn't matter what anyone else says.

This is one of the great things about design; at the end of the day it is rooted in self-expression and happiness, and this is different for each of us.

It is important that you approach design decisions in this order, because there is a process in making these decisions, it is not arbitrary. There are so many options to consider, the question must be asked: How do I know what is right for me? I think a lot of people struggle with this, so I am going to break it down.

There are a couple of key questions that you need to answer (honestly) to yourself, and only after you reach this point can you loosen up and make the actual decisions. This way, you know you are making informed decisions, and not illogical ones.

When I am putting materials and finishes together, I always ask these three simple questions:

1. **Is it suitable?**

   This usually has a clear answer and you should listen to it, even if you don't like the answer. This is a key trait of all good designers, they objectively figure things out before going any further with the design process. Everything comes after this decision.

2. **What do I like?**

   This can be anything from colour, texture, feel or style. Don't overthink it – the aim here is to get to the guts of what you actually like or dislike. Pick up something and tell yourself quickly if you like it or not. Remember, we all like different things and, at the end of the day, if you don't like something, you just don't like it, and you may never come to like it. This response to certain materials or finishes is guttural, and you need to look for what elicits a positive response in you. You are better embracing this reaction and using it as a start point for the decisions you will make. If you are finding it difficult to choose then look at other criteria which might help you make a decision, such as cost or durability.

3. **Is it within budget?**

   Every project has a budget, big or small – this shouldn't compromise your design, it should inform it. I always tell my clients that regardless of their budget, the quality of thought and design should always be there. It doesn't matter if I am designing a €5,000 kitchen or a €50,000 kitchen, the process is the same and the design imprint is always present.

These three questions should be answered in this order. When you have evaluated what you like, and decided whether it is suitable or not, then look at whether it falls within your budget.

Of course, I will now totally contradict myself! Sometimes, this process goes a little astray, and this is fine, as long as you have gone through the process in the first place – because at least you know you are breaking the rules and that this will have an impact somewhere else. For example, I have used extremely expensive and impractical materials on kitchen worktops because the client simply fell in love with a certain material (I think it was a honed slate). The love was so strong that the client was willing to make sacrifices to have this material – including adjustments to her kitchen practice such as regular oiling, etc. – but she was happy to make these sacrifices to accommodate the worktop.

So you *can* throw the above questions out the window if you want to, but you need to make sure you understand the implications of design.

The design stages overview

If you are going to work with an architect, from start to finish, then it is worth knowing the different design stages of bigger design projects, such as extensions. Actually, even if you do it yourself, you should follow these stages, as it's the tried and tested way of slowly adding layers of detail to initial ideas to ensure total clarity in design, and total clarity of information for construction.

The aim of this process is to start from a wide position, where you can see the big picture, and you can try a few ideas to see what will work best for you. Sometimes, you need to look at ideas in detail before discounting them, which can confirm that another design is actually the best thing for you.

Then, you zoom in, adding layers of detail as you go, until you have zoomed in completely, with drawings at 1:1 scale, and you're ready to build.

This process is how you minimise stress, how you manage a project from start to finish and how you ensure you avoid any common pitfalls. It's all about information and communication. It is something I explain over and over again to clients on the phone and when I meet them for the first time. Each and every stage is vital – though for different reasons.

Stage 1: Initial design

This is the stage that will involve a lot of sketches and exploration of different ideas, and is absolutely crucial as it sets out the framework for what the project will be. This gives you time to look at the different options in conjunction with your own brief, in order to decide on the best way forward in terms of design, budget and lifestyle. Sometimes, you need to look at a number of options in order to make sure you are making the right choice, and an informed choice.

This stage is like standing at a crossroads – whatever path you set off on from here, there is no going back, so you need to make sure you're heading in the right direction.

If you are planning an extension, it's all about the big moves – where the rooms are going, where the windows will be, what size it will be. You can engage a quantity surveyor at this stage to do a provisional cost estimation to make sure things are on track with budget if you need to.

Design: ODKM Architects;
Image: Barbara Egan

Stage 2: Developed design and planning

This stage develops the initial design further, and will take things to the next level. The ideas agreed in Stage 1 will be clarified, spaces become more rationalised, materials come into play, and any legislative issues will be discussed. The end of this stage is the submission of a planning application.

Stage 3: Detailed design and tender

When your planning permission comes through (all being well), it is time to detail things even further.

This is when construction detail starts to come into play, so it is a crucial stage as it will clearly mark out what materials are being used for wall, floor and roof build-ups. Construction is becoming more regulated every year, and your building will have to comply with planning as well as building regulations, so the detail in this stage will ensure that what you are building will be in accordance with the current regulations, and that it can be certified by a professional.

In addition to this, electrical and plumbing layouts will be agreed and you will start to decide on the design and specification of finished items, such as lighting, kitchen units, floor finishes and bathroom fixtures. These can become very detailed very quickly, so it is a key stage as it is effectively a shopping list for the builder to price from. It will also get you thinking about just how many decisions need to be made, and how costs can quickly escalate. This is why I always advise anyone to put a cost plan in place from day one, for everything, so you have a clear picture as to how much you want, or can, spend, and where that spend should be.

During this stage, depending on the complexity of your project, subconsultants may need to be appointed, such as a structural engineer. When completed, you will have a detailed set of architectural and structural drawings and specifications from which the contractor can price accurately, so you can invite tenders and compare builders' prices from a good base level that you know covers the work and construction that is required.

Design: ODKM Architects; Image: Barbara Egan

Stage 4: Construction and certification

Realistically, this is the most important stage because everything you have been working towards now comes into play, and the prices agreed at tender will be due at this time. The sums of money can be vast, so it's no surprise that stress levels escalate during this stage, especially when problems occur. All you can do is stick to the tender information as far as you can, and keep changes to a minimum.

Your architect will draw up a construction contract that you and the builder will sign – and this is the be-all and end-all on site. It represents the agreement between all parties to build what has been agreed for the agreed price, so every decision, every delay, change or discrepancy will be referenced back to the tender documents, and will be managed and administered through that contract. It contains every clause conceivable to deal with the common issues of construction. It will be administered by your architect to make sure things keep moving forward, unless someone is in breach of the contract (this can be you as well as the contractor!). The contract provides peace of mind, for everyone, so never start building without one.

Changes on site when certain constructed elements have already been completed generally cost money, so you always need to be one step ahead of the building process and flag any potential issues before the builder puts them in. It's easier to change the position of a door opening before it's in. This can be a really enjoyable process, where you see and are involved in the transformation of your home, and this is why having a good trusting relationship with your architect is key.

recessed light.

Art!

Vintage wall lights.

Large mirror

Concealed cistern.

Closed storage.

open storage to sink

Polished plaster.

STYLEBOOK

layout

Rich Teal

Gatsby Blue

light

Flaked Almond

Cookie Dough

Parisian Cream

Dreamy Truffle

Where to start

The Brief

Agathia Green

Windows

Flooring

LIFESTYLE

Cost, time & quantity

Orientation

A CLEAR DESIGN BRIEF =
Better Results

Fabric first

Duckegg Delight   Pistachio

Rich Teal   Satire

budget

timeline   objectives

investment   extra space

quality ← *Design* → lifestyle

Brief

family ←   → future proofing

wish list   → function

types of rooms

fabric, finishes and function

Before we start looking at individual rooms and spaces, it's worth talking about fabrics and finishes.

Style can often be a real stumbling block that paralyses many people – they have a fear of not really knowing what their style is, and as a result they play it far too safe. The tendency can be to stick to the simple generic options that offer little in terms of style or design. However, I have seen many clients take this option and they sometimes end up spending more than if they put some careful thought into what they really want. As I have said already, everyone has an idea about style, whether they know it or not.

I am a big believer in looking at style after the logical design process but, sometimes, you just have to make a call on it early and say, 'Yes, this is going to be a botanic-themed dining room – I don't care, I love it.' If you feel strongly towards a certain style – one that relates to you on some level – then that is fine, regardless if it's 'correct' in the space or not. After all, design is all about being happy in your home.

I see different reactions to different styles, and sometimes it baffles me. If we live in a period 1930s house, should we decorate it of the same era? If so, should we dress in 1930s clothing as well? The answer is of course no (unless you want to). The same logic follows through for the opposite end of the spectrum – a modernist home does not have to be filled with contemporary furniture; period antiques can sit very well in a modern aesthetic.

Designers are obsessed with the things we touch. While we all love things that look great, how something feels is often what separates the mundane from the sublime.

I'm talking everything – from door handles, bathroom taps, handrails, light switches right through to the kitchen sink, literally. They are also permanent items, hence 'fixed', and this is another reason why they're so important. It is worth putting a bit extra into the finishes, because something like an extra-special kitchen tap can really elevate an ordinary kitchen.

It's small touches that are clever because by pushing the boat out a little on a beautiful tap, you can make a simple kitchen look and feel all the more luxurious, and, for me, that's clever design. You might look at the price of the tap in isolation and think it's too expensive, but in the overall picture, it could be the best spend you make on the kitchen.

The options in terms of finish, design and cost are as varied and vast as anything you can imagine, so it really comes back to style and value versus cost. Sometimes, however, you may simply fall in love with a particular fitting and decide that you're willing to stretch to its cost.

FLOORS

The finish on your floors is another of the key elements in the fabric part of any building, and another big driver in terms of style and feel. It can be the largest decorative feature in any space, and can also be one of the most expensive, but like I say, fabric first – this is something that you need to think about. The spectrum of materials is vast, so start with the practicalities of what you are trying to achieve, and when you have those sorted, you can start to play with choice.

Timber

You can't beat timber. It has been the staple choice for floors for decades and for good reason. It has countless styles and finishes, and adds warmth and character like no other material. It can also add a heightened sense of luxury as it is a sensual material, it's close to nature and is familiar to all of us.

It's also extremely versatile and can be used anywhere in the home – including in the kitchen and in bathrooms, no matter what anyone else tells you. A simple oil or wax finish and good installation is all you need. Personally, I think the characteristics of a timber floor really shine through in these spaces, where we usually have the obligatory tile finish. My advice would be to accept a certain level of marking with any timber floor. I think this adds to their character; they are not intended to be as flawless as a porcelain tile, so go with the flow if this suits your style. Always make sure your timber comes from selected sustainable sources.

Timber floor designs

While the straight-and-narrow format of laying timber holds true, wooden floors have far more potential for variety than you may think. If they are cut into smaller pieces and arranged in patterns, they can be every bit as intricate and detailed as tiling. When the design is done correctly, it can elevate your timber floor to a whole new level. Even in board form, there are variations that are worth exploring, and it is a great example of how important texture can be in design.

As a general note, the more intricate the pattern, the more expensive it will be. If the design requires different types of wood, more cuts and measurements, and more time to install, then the cost will obviously reflect this. With intricate work, craftsmanship counts – you need to ensure you hire a skilled and experienced professional if your design is very detailed.

There are three main types of timber floors available:

Solid timber:
Perhaps the ultimate in timber floor finishes is the solid timber floor. This has timber all the way through and can be re-sanded countless times to bring the finish back to life. They are generally the most expensive choice because of the quality of the wood. Just ensure that the wood has been acclimatised to its environment, and you allow it to sit on site for around thirty days prior to installation. This ensures all the moisture has been drawn out of the wood so that it doesn't warp. The installation should be carried out by a specialist if possible.

Semi-solid engineered timber:
This type of timber flooring has a layer of solid timber fixed on top of another cheaper material, like plywood. It can still be every bit as expensive as a solid timber floor because of the extra engineering, which gives it increased strength and stability, and limits its susceptibility to warping. For this reason, some people think it is a better option if the floor is being installed over a new concrete screed with underfloor heating; however, I have used both this and solid timber and can see no difference between the two if the solid timber floor is installed correctly.

Laminate floors:

I've included laminate floors with timber floors, despite laminate having very little timber, because they're installed in the same way as timber floors and can achieve the same type of look. I think laminate flooring has improved dramatically in the past few years. It is a thin veneer of timber fixed onto a cheap, synthetic material, such as MDF, which makes it an ideal, cost-effective solution if your budget is tight. While it will never compare to either a solid or semi-solid floor, in finish or longevity, it can get you out of a problem area quickly and cheaply.

Straight boards

With a straight board, there are still options in terms of installation, orientation, width and length that will impact on how the space in which it is laid feels. You can install boards parallel or perpendicular to walls or units to lead the eye or create a boardwalk-type feeling in a room. Generally speaking, the boardwalk arrangement will visually help widen a space and the straight option will narrow it. In addition to this, you have choices in width of the boards and whether or not to keep the same width throughout or have different widths arranged together. Random-width flooring patterns were born out of necessity because early floor planks were milled from the entire log, which meant you were left with different-width boards. These days, this is much more of a design statement and most designers commonly use planks of three different widths in a repeating pattern.

Single-width boards are ideal for clean, linear, modern spaces as they give a sense of uniformity. This is not as fussy as the random-width design, and the boards are available in a range of widths. This style is at its best with an extra wide board, up to 10 inches in some cases, and can give a very solid aesthetic to the finish.

Different looks can be achieved by playing with board lengths, and this is done to add a little visual interest and intricacy to the timber. You can have boards of the same length laid in an offset manner or you can have different-length boards laid randomly. Usually the joints are all staggered to reduce the chance of a continuous joint line appearing in the room. This is a decision you can make based solely on what you look you prefer.

Diagonal

To create a diagonal pattern, the boards are installed parallel to each other at a 45-degree (or similar) angle to the walls. This is a great choice for smaller rooms as it can alter the proportions of the room and make it look bigger, because the eye is drawn diagonally to the corner of the rooms and not to the flat surfaces of the walls. Sometimes in a small space you can get away with something like this a lot more easily than you would in a larger room.

Parquet

Parquet is any design that involves a geometric pattern of angular wood pieces put together in a particular style. These designs flourished during the Renaissance and range from the simple to the wonderfully complex. Intricate parquet patterns carry

Chevron:

This is a really cool pattern, where equal board lengths meet point to point creating a continuous zigzag effect, which looks like long strips of diagonals (see pages 35/40).

Herringbone:

For this, the wood blocks finish perpendicular to each other, and they are arranged in a repeated pattern resulting in a broken zigzag. This removes the strong linear element you see in chevron flooring (see below).

the names of the seventeenth-century palaces where they were developed, such as Versailles and Bordeaux, and I love timber floors finished in this way. This style was popular in nineteenth-century Paris, where many of the apartments from that time feature parquet floors in either the herringbone or chevron pattern.

Basketweave

The key to this style is in its name. It creates the illusion that the boards are woven together like a basket. There are a range of designs, but each one will add a lovely patchwork quality to the floor. It is especially useful over a large area where you may want some variety and texture in the floor to break up the space.

Picture frame

This design features a border around the main floor, often created using the same wood as the main floor but placed parallel to the walls, with a strip of wood (or a different finish colour) added to define the frame. This is a much more formal edge detail that can help define a room shape.

Stone

Natural stone is the next choice for an enduring floor finish and, like timber, the choices available are endless. Its properties are all about strength, honesty and durability, and yet this is coupled with an amazing array of colour and textural options. This means it looks amazing and is also very practical, which makes it an obvious choice for flooring and wall finishes in bathrooms, kitchens and for worktops.

Stone is a natural material and there is often variety within each batch quarried, so you should always expect changes in colour and pattern throughout. This is part of its charm and character, and what makes it so appealing.

The same principles of design apply to stone as they do to anything else, and there are countless options available in both the dimensions and layouts of the stone to create interesting effects. Regardless of the stone you choose, always ask the supplier about any specific treatments that are required to the different stone finishes as these can vary drastically between products.

Honed:
This is a finish where the stone is buffed to a degree to give it a dull matt shine, which makes it almost velvet to touch. Designers love the look and feel of this finish as it is so tactile.

Flamed:
This is where an intense flame is applied to the surface of the stone, causing it to become rough. It is an ideal finish for exterior applications where slip resistance is an important factor. This finish cannot be applied to all stone surfaces so check if it's possible with the stone you would like to use.

Sandblasted:
A high-pressure jet of siliceous sand or steel shots is applied to the area being treated. This produces a smooth abrasion, leaving the material with a slightly scratched but not rugged surface.

Polished:
This is where the stone is buffed to the maximum, giving a glossy and shiny finish. All of which adds a rich, deep and luxurious element to the final product.

Chiselled:
This is a rougher finish, ideal for anti-slip purposes, so a great way to use stone outside on terraces and patio areas.

A number of options are available in terms of the finish and each gives a very different look and feel to the material. I've detailed the five most common types on the previous page.

You should also think about the stone you would like to use. Different types of stone lend themselves to different applications depending on the durability, feel and finish you would like. Listed below are six of my favourite types of stone.

Slate:
I love slate. I have used it on floors and kitchen worktops, and its versatility means it has been utilised as a building stone for centuries. It's naturally thinner than other stones, and its dark tones make it a perfect natural and dramatic floor finish.

Limestone:
The colours in limestone are generally bright, varying in off-whites and soft greys. It's a stone that can be used inside and out, with different finishes giving way to different properties. If it is being used externally, ask for a 'chiselled' finish, which will increase its anti-slip properties.

Marble:
There is a creamy, liquid quality to marble that just makes is so lovely to touch. Again, don't forget to ask about specific treatments as some types of marble need a sealant.

Granite:
Generally on the darker side of the spectrum, granite is rock hard and extremely durable. Being quite granular in texture, it's completely different to the fluidity of marble. ▶

Concrete:

Polished concrete floors have become very popular in recent years. Even though concrete is essentially a fairly crude structural building material, when you polish away at the surface, you expose all the stone aggregate in the mix. The result is a beautifully layered and naturally glossy floor finish that is every bit as handsome as stone, but at a more affordable price. It's a bit like baking a cake – you choose the colour of the base (the concrete), adding pigments to change the colour if you wish, and then you pick the aggregate. This can be a basic stone mix or can include marble or glass chippings (which is more of a terrazzo floor). Either way, a polished concrete floor has evolved out of the industrial units and is now firmly on the designer's wish list for the most luxurious of homes.

Again, this is a natural floor finish and it will not be uniform in appearance. It will swirl where different stone clusters have gathered, so if you want a uniform floor finish, don't go for concrete. Make sure to install expansion joints around every 5 square metres to prevent larger cracking, but hairline cracks are inevitable so you need to make sure you like the appearance before you commit.

We have also specified power-floated concrete floors, which is a cheaper alternative again. This omits the expensive polishing process in favour of just smoothing the concrete over. You can paint it or leave it in its natural state but, either way, you get something that looks amazing at a fraction of the cost of an expensive stone or timber floor.

Tiles:

Decorative patterned tiling and floor design can be a great way to add vibrancy and texture to a room. I think the real beauty of a tile finish is encapsulated in the texture and refinement they introduce, which is especially good in smaller spaces. Tiles can add a layer of detail and texture like no other material. This is why you see a lot of mosaic tiles in en-suites, which also give you an anti-slip element – always useful in a bathroom!

Carpet

I have to talk about carpet, because I am tired of seeing people discard it in favour of timber time and time again without stopping to remember how sinking your toes into the soft heavy pile of a carpet can be utterly splendid.

In the right environment, carpet is a terrific floor finish, and has been for centuries. From a practical perspective, it is an excellent insulator of sound and heat, and from a comfort level, it gives a warmth that is ideally suited to the more private and secluded places in our homes, like bedrooms and living rooms. Even if you don't want a carpet finish anywhere, at the very least get some rugs in. We have installed large-scale carpets over timber floors, leaving just a 400–500 mm timber border around the edge. This gave the best of both worlds, and it looked great. It's a useful solution to arguments about whether to carpet or timber the living-room floor. It's also a good option if you are particularly sensitive to dust, which a carpet will hold regardless of how aggressively you clean it.

Mixing timber floors with large rugs is a great way to layer the flooring in a room. It looks great, and it's soft on your feet.

Design/Image: Dulux (Night Jewels 1 & Azure Fusion 1)

Cork:

Believe it or not, cork is a natural and environmentally friendly material that is a good substitute for wood flooring. It is soft and warm underfoot, and comes in both tiles and boards, so you can play around with the installation in much the same way as you can with timber. It's also very sustainable, as it is a renewable and recyclable resource.

Vinyl:

Vinyl is back, in music and in design. Forget everything you know about your granny's old kitchen floor, vinyl is now more durable and desirable than ever. While, on the one hand, its durability is a positive, environmentally it is a negative as it doesn't biodegrade. However, innovation with the product in the design sense has led to some serious improvements in this regard, and its popularity continues to grow.

Rubber:

If you have ever walked on a rubber floor you'll know that it feels great. Soft and spongy, yet slip resistant and durable, it ticks a lot of boxes. It can be fitted as tiles or sheets, and, in larger areas, you can achieve a seamless finish with a poured synthetic rubber floor. Who would have thought it would look so good!

Linoleum:

Better known as lino, this is a sustainable, durable and high-quality flooring material and its versatility enables designers to pick and choose from an endless array of colours and designs.

Design/Image: Dulux (Caribbean Dawn 3, Kiwi Burst 3 & African Adventure 3)

Alternative floor coverings

As well as the classic floor options above, there are more and more alternative options for flooring that can be practical and cost-effective and yet utterly beautiful.

I've detailed opposite the four most popular alternative materials used to cover floors.

WINDOWS

Every architect is either openly or secretly obsessed with windows because they play such a significant role in defining an internal space and connecting buildings to their surroundings. Done right, they can add serious drama. They're also a very expensive item so it is worth considering the options, and really getting involved in choosing the style and finish. This goes back to my 'Fabric First' mantra – windows are something you should only do once, so making the right decision is critical. The choice of finish will have an impact on the internal finishes, so take your time to think through the options.

Depending on your overall budget, something as simple as changing your windows can drastically change a room and, more often than not, they are first on the list of things to be done if an existing house is being refurbished.

Windows don't have to be a certain size – technological progress has ensured that if you can think it, you can make it. Large openings, pivot doors, frameless glass – if you can't afford to build on any extra space, changing your window size and design is the first thing to look at.

"Windows are something you should only do once, so making the right decision is critical."

You do need to be careful if the windows you are changing are to the front of your house; if the changes are significant, they may require planning permission. Always check with the local authority if you want to do something to the front of the house.

Big picture windows are great. They let in light, they dissolve walls and boundaries, they make narrow spaces feel bigger, and they bring nature and the great outdoors right into the heart of your home. Cost is an issue, but windows have such an impact and effect on the internal space that you should put as much as you can into your window redesign – you will never regret it. This really highlights what I mean by cost versus value. A small space with a big sliding door is so much better than a small space with a small window in the end wall. At the end of the day, it's the same space, but the sliding door makes the space something special.

As always, know where the sun comes from and understand your orientation. Where should the windows go? How will it affect the use of the room? Get these decisions right first and then you can think about style and colour – as these are major factors in how a room will look and feel.

There are four main types of window finish.

Design/Image: Carson & Crushell Architects

Aluminium windows:
As the name suggests, these are made entirely from aluminium. They offer good strength and performance values, as well as endless colour options based on the RAL colour chart system (an industry standard colour matching system to ensure like for like colouring). With aluminium windows you can push the limits and increase size openings, enabling a greater range of choice in your window design.

Timber windows:
When I think of timber windows, I think of my dad endlessly repainting our single-glazed windows thirty years ago. Thankfully, this chore is no more. The manufacture and design of timber windows has progressed so much since then that a new timber window today is now energy-efficient and low maintenance. With beautiful detailing, a hardwood timber window can add a lot of character and warmth to a space.

Aluclad windows:
This type of window is for those who want the high performance and zero maintenance of aluminium on the outside, and all the warmth of timber on the inside. Endless colour options are available for the outside as well, and the timber on the inside can be left natural, or you can varnish or paint it.

uPVC windows:
These are not the most environmentally friendly choice, but they are the least expensive. They perform as well as the other options, but I would generally only specify uPVC when the budget available is at an absolute minimum.

Positioning a window in the right location draws in natural rays of sunshine, and makes the spaces inside feel bigger and brighter. Seeing the sky from inside your home is a beautiful thing.

Think about your window frame design and size. Here, there is no frame at all at the corner – a glass-to-glass joint is used to make the corner disappear. This, combined with large glass panels and slim frames, makes the room feel part of the garden. This is why window design is critical.

LIGHTING

Lighting is what sets a mood in a room, and I am obsessed by it. I have OCD with lighting and have been known to enter people's living rooms and change the light settings … while they are sitting on the sofa. Lighting can relax you instantly, or it can stress you out.

If you find that a particular room is bothering you, ask yourself: Is the lighting right? Chances are, it's not. The age of the four downlighters in a room is dead, as is the 'big main light' in the middle of the ceiling. You can design your lighting every bit as much as the rest of your house, and when you do it right it will absolutely transform your home.

Lighting design is all about making you feel a certain way. Whether you want to chill out, dance, watch television, eat, sleep, have friends over to dinner or waste away a Sunday afternoon, the lighting in a room will affect how naturally and easily these things happen.

First things first, though: there are a number of different types of lighting that you should understand.

Lighting is all about layering, and it is as much about darkness and shadow as it is about light. Without doubt, this is one of the most important elements in any project, big or small.

Ambient lighting:

Ambient, or general, lighting provides an area with overall illumination and it should provide a comfortable level of brightness, enabling you to perform tasks and move about safely. Ceiling or wall-mounted fixtures, recessed or track lights, and floor and table lamps can be used for this type of lighting. In short, this is the main ceiling light and recessed spotlights we see everywhere. I call this the emergency lighting – what you would turn on if there was a fire and you had to evacuate. As a tip, I always put the main ambient lighting on dimmer switches as this gives you full control of the mood of a room when you need to turn on the big light.

Task lighting:

This helps you perform specific tasks and activities, such as reading, writing or cooking, and is usually achieved with recessed and track lighting, pendant lighting, portable lamps, or desk lamps. This should be free of distracting glare but bright enough to be used without any ambient lighting if needs be. This type of lighting is best summed up by the light above your seat on an aeroplane; it illuminates your book perfectly but everyone else can still sleep. Always make sure your task lighting is on a separate loop to the other lights so that they can be operated independently.

Accent lighting:

This is a concentrated focus of light to create a visual point of interest, and is typically used to highlight architectural features, paintings, plants, sculptures or collectables. It is usually achieved by using track, recessed or wall-mounted fixtures – as well as large recessed spotlights in the ceiling which can be angled onto a wall. This type of lighting adds an extra layer to a room, and is the equivalent of the light that shines on public buildings and landmarks.

Different types of lighting all doing different jobs. Function comes first (as it should) and the style of light comes after.

WALLS

We don't really live in modular box rooms anymore. We want flexibility and openness when we need it, and we want seclusion and privacy as well. How we live and what we ask of our homes has changed. We need different spaces in order to live differently and, for this reason, everything we know about domesticity has to be rethought.

In open-plan living, the need for walls has completely disappeared, giving way to something much more fluid and interactive. It questions how we break up space and to what degree. Walls are no longer surfaces with standard sized openings in them, they can be much more sculptural, and still do the same job.

Wall finishes can be every bit as elaborate as those for floors, and are a key factor in setting the tone and feeling of a room. They define our space, so we are intuitively responsive to their characteristics. This means the considered treatment of the walls around you is fundamental in dealing with problem spaces that might be too small or too cold.

Paint

Paint is great. It's the most accessible and cheapest form of wall decoration, and there are endless colours and finishes to choose from. And if you don't like it when you're finished, you can always paint over it.

Colour is a powerful thing. It is the biggest single driver of mood in the design world, and can psychologically alter how a space is experienced and perceived. It plays a role in the overall palette that makes up a space or a room. It is a bit like a soloist playing in an orchestra – it can rise above the music, it can scream at you, or it can blend in and be almost unheard. In either case, it affects you whether or not you know it.

Colour can also visually alter a space. You can pull surfaces closer to you or push them away – all through the manipulation of different tones of colour. This is particularly useful if you have a long, narrow room, perhaps it is more oblong than square. It is also useful in narrow spaces, where although you can't make the space bigger, you can make sure it feels bigger.

As a general rule, darker colours will be more upfront and appear closer to you. A dark-coloured floor will appear grounded and will enable the walls and ceiling, in lighter colours, to lift upwards from the ground floor, giving the appearance that the floor-to-ceiling heights are greater than they actually are. This is why everyone

Design/Images: Dulux (Blush Noisette 4/ Pamplona Purple 4/ Cherished Gold)

Top tip for choosing paint colours

Test, test, test … I cannot stress how important it is to test paint colours properly in your home. No matter what the colours look like in colour cards, a paint shop or in someone else's house, the lighting in your home will ultimately dictate how the colour will appear, so testing properly is really important. This is particularly true for greys, which are notoriously difficult to get right. I always recommend to brush the colour out onto a piece of A4 card and test it in the lightest and darkest part of the room in both natural and artificial light. Trust me, if you do this you will avoid arguments!

paints their ceilings white. If you paint your ceiling a darker colour, it feels like it is a lot closer to you, and you become much more aware of its presence – useful in larger spaces with overly high ceilings.

The same rule applies to the walls, so in a narrow hallway, the safe bet is to go with a lighter tone on the walls, with a darker floor finish to optimise the impression that it is bigger than it is.

When considering your overall colour scheme, given that the options are endless, a piece of advice is to put a mood board together where you put all the materials and colours you are thinking of using on one board, together, side by side. This will give you the overall big picture, so keep it up to date as it will highlight any conflicts in your choices as they arise.

Wallpaper

Where do we start with wallpaper? I rarely use it, but when I do it gives an added depth and dimension to a room that can be anything you want it to be – striking, calming, serene or insane. It can get you out of a tight spot when you need something with punch and it can add a layer of glamour to a room like nothing else.

My advice is to disregard most of what you know about wallpaper. We've all heard of it, but forget the 'feature wall' idea. This doesn't work, and was never really anything other than a passing term used on home improvement television shows. If

(Left) Design: Tilestyle; Image: Dúra Photography; (Right) © Shutterstock/scenery2

Decorative tiles and wallpaper play a role in creating the mood you want in a room. They add texture or colour if that's what's needed, and they can be as subtle or as crazy as you like.

you are going to wallpaper, do so with conviction and do the full room. You can break it up under picture rails, or use it in a more contemporary way in bands or in storage units, but whatever way you wallpaper, make sure you go for it. Either keep it simple or be bold. There is no in between for me.

Costs can spiral out of control for the more luxurious brands and finishes, so, again, weigh up the value versus the cost if wallpaper is your preferred option.

Tiles

We mostly use tiles in kitchens and bathrooms, but they are more versatile than this, with a huge range of finishes.

The first decision you need to make is whether to opt for ceramic or porcelain. Porcelain is the more expensive option because the colour goes through the tile. After this, you need to think about pattern.

Tiles don't need to be large, bland slabs fixed to a bathroom floor. The quality and variety available means that tiles are an ideal way to introduce some intricacy and detail into the overall design palette. Using tiles is one of the main ways that you can complement colours and textures in a detailed and delicate way to really lift a room.

Polished plaster

We are used to seeing polished plaster in hotels, particularly in Italy where it originated, but it is also creeping into the residential market, and it is easy to see why. The finish can vary from a high polish that looks like marble to velvet smooth, almost dusty, all giving a continuous, seamless effect that looks and feels top end.

In fact, the technology is ever-changing, and the same techniques can be used to create bespoke stone and concrete finishes, with endless colours, designs and finishes available. I have used it in bathrooms and living rooms, and every time I see it I love it.

Timber

There is no need to think of your walls as a standard plasterboard skim finish. The variety of finishes we see for flooring can also be applied to walls, and none more so than timber. Plywood is a fine and handsome material, and much loved by designers across the globe. It is cheap, durable and extremely beautiful. If you don't fancy another painted internal wall, line it with timber to give it a different look.

Glass

Painted glass has been around for decades but it's still a relatively cost-effective way of achieving great-looking results on a budget. It creates depth, and this is a key tool designers use to add layers to a space, and stop it from becoming one-dimensional and flat.

It's great on kitchen splashbacks, or at the back of a built-in bookshelf to give it that extra depth. If the colour is subtle, or better still matches the wall colour, then you get a very understated but high-end finish that costs a lot less than it looks.

Mirror

The benefits of using mirrors are well known, as mirrors bounce light and increase depth. You can reflect outdoor space, windows or entire rooms with one that is positioned appropriately. You can apply a mirror finish to an entire wall, or doorway, to play a trick on the eye in terms of depth, but there's also something a bit bling and luxurious about using mirrors. Used in the right way, a mirror can do more than make a space look bigger.

DOORS

If we are going to rethink our living spaces, a good place to start is with doors. They have been caught up in a race to the bottom, and the result is that most of us instinctively think of a door as a nothing more than a 900-mm wide 2,100-mm high, domestic piece of standard timber. But if we don't necessarily need to live in modular box rooms, then why should we negotiate different rooms and spaces through such modest clunky objects?

Of course we need separation between certain spaces, but surely there are other, better ways to achieve this?

I have completed a number of projects where the walls were broken up to act as sculptural objects intersecting a combination of rooms – with no doors at all. It may sound weird, but when people visit, they move around so freely and openly that they don't actually realise there are no doors.

This is the ease by which good design can help us to live … when done right, you don't really notice it at all. It should be easy. It's when it's wrong that bad design is noticed, because something is too small or it bangs off something or it won't close properly.

The great Ludwig Mies van der

"The great Ludwig Mies van der Rohe said it better than I ever could: less really is more."

Rohe said it better than I ever could: less really is more. I have often found that there are only ever one or two core ideas behind anything, so if you are struggling with information overload, strip everything back to its basics and keep it simple. Do a couple of things really well, instead of a number of things half-well. Wall finish, floor finish, lighting design and a couple of smart touches or pieces of furniture here and there will solve most problem areas – so don't overthink things.

THINKING OUTSIDE THE BOX

When you have a handle on the basics above, and you're in a good place to tackle the design head on, then you need to think about where you're going to start. This means understanding what is going to influence your designs. Leonardo da Vinci said that 'simplicity is the ultimate in sophistication' and he was right. Keep it simple.

The great stock of Georgian architecture in Ireland is something to be proud of. We could learn a few lessons from the Georgians, particularly in the nature of the spaces they created. Room size, height and volume were generous, and are still as impressive today as they were when built.

Standard ceiling heights that we see everywhere now are 2.4 metres and they have become de rigueur. This is something that I hope changes because there is so much drama to be had when ceiling heights increase, or disappear completely. Double-height spaces and voids are an amazing way to interconnect spaces vertically in a building, and bring in light from different areas.

Design: Maxime Laroussi/Urban Agency; Image: Barbara Egan

63

Design: Studio Red Architects; Image: Peter Grogan / Emagine

1. **Wall finishes**

   Using timber as a wall finish
   here places focus on the
   fireplace, but also adds warmth
   and texture to the rooms.

2. **Simple layouts**

   Simple layouts and furniture
   make for great, usable spaces.

3. **Window design**

   Full height, up to the ceiling,
   capturing the views and
   breaking boundaries between
   what is inside and outside.

4. **Varying ceiling heights**

   This is a great way to break up
   open-plan spaces, as it helps
   define different zones within
   one large space.

We all want spaces that lift our spirits, and we have forgotten that a high ceiling is possibly the best way to achieve this. It increases the drama and dynamic of a space in a way nothing else can. I think we associate added space with added value, and sometimes this can close off options like this. It's too easy to say 'Can we not use it for another bedroom?', but putting this kind of height into your home adds so much more value than having another small room.

So if you have a spare box room that's just collecting dust and clutter, think about how dramatic your downstairs space would look if you took out that room and opened the space upwards. You'll need to make sure your style choices marry with the practical goals of your brief but, again, if you have a clear sense of what you want, decisions on the fundamentals will be more straightforward.

The thing to remember with style is that you need to choose your own style and then really go for it.

CREATIVITY

None of the above practical considerations should stifle your creativity, or your inspiration. People should demand more from their homes, and they should want more. Having a tight budget is a challenge but it doesn't have to inhibit creativity in ways to tackle different problems.

A detailed and realistic design brief sets the framework for what you want, and as long as you stick to your brief, you'll be fine.

A lot of people seem to think this is beyond them, but we are all creative creatures; look at any toddler and you'll see that stimulating creativity is something anyone can do. Being creative in the places we spend most of our time can really add a tangible value to our quality of life – and,

"Being creative in the places we spend most of our time can really add a tangible value to our quality of life."

if you do feel uncertain about your creativity, just remember that creativity can be taught, and therefore it can be learned.

The act of designing starts with openly questioning the brief, without seeking identifiable solutions or tangible outcomes. It's open and playful. The answers will come in time but the first step is to just challenge it. I know this might sound contradictory, but the idea is to challenge your preconceived ideas – think of it as a stress test. This is the magic of the creative process, because it will force you to think really hard about what you need and what you want – especially if you have to start making compromises to marry this up with the budget.

For example, a request I see every day is the need for 'more space'. This may or may not actually mean extending or knocking down walls. It may just mean that there is a lack of usable space … and there could be a whole lot of different approaches and answers to this, all within the existing footprint.

The first step is to *challenge* that statement in an open and honest way, to kick around some ideas. Analyse the current setup in your house. How efficient is the setup? How are all the spaces used? Why are they used in certain ways? Why do you need more space? More often than not, you can identify problems in one area that have a ripple effect somewhere else in the house. So the answer isn't always where you think it might be. At a very basic level, designing is problem solving.

AUDIT

Last but not least, I want to talk about the self-audit. This is not sexy, but it is the most important piece of advice I give to almost every single client, regardless of the size of the project or the brief: DECLUTTER, NOW!

Any house, it doesn't matter, can always trim away a good 20–30 per cent of stuff that is just taking up too much space. We need to throw out a lot more stuff. Be ruthless. Keep the wedding album obviously, but get rid of the junk, it's holding you back.

THE RULES

All these things – fabric, finish and function – will give you a starting point for how to approach changing your home for the better using the power of design.

The design brief makes it easy for you to figure out the problems you're facing, what you want and how you should approach your project.

Double height spaces add so much drama, light and grandeur to a room that is totally unique, and impossible to replicate. There is nothing more calming than a sense of openness.

Architect: Darragh Lynch Architects; Image: Donal Murphy Photography

Design: Kingston Lafferty Design; Image: Donal Murphy Photography

Key decisions on the fundamentals

Design brief:
This is the blueprint for the task at hand.
Ask questions, then ask some more.

Fabric first:
Get the big moves right and invest in
big-ticket items – mainly windows!

Form versus function:
Before you think about what it looks like,
make sure it works.

Layout:
It all starts here. Get this right and everything
else will be easier.

Lighting (natural and artificial):
This sets the mood of a space. It's not a
luxury, it's a necessity.

Be creative:
Try not to let restrictions stifle you too much.

Fixtures:
Push the boat out a little here, it can make all
the difference.

I've called these guidelines 'The Rules', but they are less stringent than that. It's more of a guide to show you how to ask yourself hard questions, and how to listen to the answers – even when they're not what you want to hear – in order to truly understand the problem so that you can tackle it head on. When you have this, you can go through all the information I've given you to examine the criteria that is most important to you to deal with the task at hand.

While the above represents a structure in establishing the design brief and thinking about how to implement it, I want to put equal weight on breaking the rules when you know what they are. I suppose this is called flair – you can look at something and have a gut feeling or idea that hasn't necessarily been part of the design-brief process, and that's fine by me. It's something that happens all the time, and it's great when it does!

The rules around doors, windows, walls and what we consider to be the 'standard' size or material should always be challenged, and broken if necessary. There is always a degree of rule bending and breaking in any design process. This can sometimes release real creativity – but it's about understanding the context and the parameters of the design, and then allowing it to grow naturally. If this means some rules are broken, then so be it. Don't fight it.

There can be a fine line between what will work and what will not, and how close to this line you are willing to go is a personal decision. Only you know how comfortable you are with creating, and living with, something that doesn't conform to the 'standard'. And remember, things sometimes work together even though they shouldn't. An example of this is rules around colour, and what colours clash (black and navy, red and pink) but I love black and navy together – it's dramatic, strong and powerful and really moody. It shouldn't work, but it does in the right situation, so don't be afraid to bend and break convention.

It's about confidence in being able to discern the difference between getting away with it … and not.

Playing it safe is sticking by the rules; if you're struggling with something, then the rules will see you through. If you are feeling brave, then tread closer to the line, and experiment.

Now that you have an idea of the bigger picture – what the layout, orientation and function of the rooms in your home are – it's time to look at each room in closer detail.

welcome to the transition

What I mean by 'transition' is any area that makes up the in-between spaces in a home. Those spaces that connect the rooms and are the glue that holds everything together – hallways, staircases, landings, corridors and entrance porches. If you really want to give your house a makeover, then starting with a hallway will add drama and a sense of completeness to the work that you're doing in the rest of the house.

I want to start with these areas because they are often the first series of spaces you will see in any building. A lobby, a staircase or an entrance hallway is usually what we are greeted with when we first walk through a door – and it *is* a greeting, so it should welcome you with a smile. These areas also set the tone for the rest of the rooms to follow. It's all about the approach, and I always know so much about a house from what I see as soon as I open the door.

Yet people forget that these spaces are rooms too. OK, you only pass through them moments at a time but they are rooms all the same – it's just that their function is different. You wouldn't watch television in a hallway but, then again, you're not supposed to. These are fleeting spaces, but you use them every day.

More often than not, they are also challenging spaces. They can be too small, too narrow or an odd shape, so I think they provide a real test for any architect or designer because you simply have to design your way around what's there and make the most of what you have.

When designing a house from scratch, this is somewhat easier because you are in full control of size, proportion and layout. But even with this, we always ensure that the connecting spaces make some sort of statement because they must embody the characteristics of the house and join it all together.

As these are the first spaces that you enter, they're a bit like going to a job interview – if the handshake doesn't go well, the rest could be a struggle. You cannot underestimate how important these spaces are.

HALLWAYS

Hallways greet you at the end of the day and welcome your visitors into your home. In ancient Greece, the entrance was about shedding layers of public life, and was quite a spiritual place. It served as an emotional transition between public and private life, and in terms of a hallway's function, that still rings true for all of us today.

And yet, hallways have lost their charm and more often than not become a narrow means to an end. This is a shame because even just a small amount of leftover

Design: Plus Architecture; Image: Donal Murphy Photography

A very simple but beautiful hallway. It is calm and elegant, but there is real quality of space here. Natural light and elongated views make for an interesting space between rooms.

space (if it's there) can be utilised to give something back to the house, and to you.

A chair in the right position, looking out a window, with a small table can become a place to sit. A bookcase built in to a wall reveal as you go up a staircase can bring huge character, tactility and life to a space that would otherwise just be a painted plaster finish. Making the most of the little spaces can actually make all the difference in the world.

The mat recessed into the durable stone floor. The built-in seat for putting on your wellies. The task lighting above, and the concealed storage for all the coats and umbrellas. Perfect function in each and every detail, yet also very cool and with a sense of personal style.

In terms of function, hallways have a difficult job to do. On one level, they must protect the privacy of the house; they can't be too open and you don't necessarily want passers-by to be able to see all the way in. Yet, they are all about being open and welcoming to whoever does walk in the door, so there is a bit of a dichotomy and there are contradicting principles at play. As always, it's all about context, and understanding what you can and can't do.

You need to look at a hallway and understand what it is. Is it too small? Too big? Does it need furniture? Would wall-mounted storage be better? Does it have to be completely uncluttered? Every space is different, so you should be aware of what will work and what won't within the space you have.

As a general rule, hallways should be unobstructed and relatively hard-wearing. They are used constantly, every day, multiple times, so through traffic needs to be considered. The floor finish should be bullet proof, as should the wall finish. Recessing a coil mat into the finished floor is a great way to make sure people wipe their feet when they come in and don't drag stones or grit into the house. Somewhere to put your keys and the mail is always useful and, depending on the size of the hallway, this could be a console table or a wall-mounted shelf – regardless of size, everything should still serve its function.

"As a general rule, hallways should be unobstructed and relatively hard-wearing."

Coats, shoes, umbrellas, etc. should be neatly stored – but they need not be completely tucked away out of site. We like to have our things around us, so it's OK to have these on view, as long as there is a space designed for them and they're not in the way. If the space is too small, the best option for this could simply be a couple of hooks for your everyday coat that you grab on your way out the door, with the rest stored somewhere else.

If your hallway is particularly small, think about small things, like the door and the handle; you can always make an impression with these if space is limited and you have to keep things super simple on the inside. In small spaces, I recommend you show your storage instead of trying to box it off. This keeps it looking 'light', adds interest and familiarity to the space, as it's all your own stuff, and it also keeps you concise in terms of outdoor wear as you don't have a whole room to throw coats into and forget about for three years. A small umbrella stand, with some coat storage, a built-in shelf and a place for keys, with a small mirror – if you have a tiny hallway, you can get something that has all of the above into one unit almost. Even at this small size, it will never be underused. It can be wall-mounted above a radiator, or the space behind the swing of a door, but either way, getting something into a leftover space in a hallway will reap huge rewards.

Mirrors are great ways to make spaces look bigger. Always try and get them on a wall opposite a window, so you will get the added benefit of an extra window without the hassle! Also, they're very useful as you walk out the door to ensure you don't have jam on your face from breakfast.

This is the essence of what I am talking about. It doesn't matter about the size or the budget of the hallway you have, the function has to be the same. You have to use your hallway, and it has to work for you.

Light can be one of the most important factors when changing the feel and tone of a hallway. In an entrance hallway, you should know where to go instinctively. It should be laid out to lead you naturally to where you want to be, which is usually to one of the primary living spaces. A guest should be able to walk in and instantly figure out where to go – and not accidentally walk into a room they shouldn't! Every element of what you put into a hallway should reinforce this, and light can be the simplest way of telling people where to go because we all follow the light.

If you can get natural light into a hallway, then do. As they can be limited spaces, sometimes this may have to come from above, as a skylight, or from the entrance door itself. It's good to have a mix of opaque and clear glass on the front door as you want to keep that balance of letting light in, but preserving privacy.

Introducing a window into the hallway can transform it, but this isn't always possible. If you have a series of doors off the hallway, then these can be replaced with glass, enabling a break in the solidity of the hallway, but still demarcating the rooms from the transition space while borrowing the light from adjoining rooms. Using a glossier floor finish can help bounce light around as well.

If you have a dark hallway, with no opportunity for natural light, then you need to embrace the power of artificial lighting, and get thinking about ways to improve the space. A well-thought-out lighting plan can create a sense of luxury and the impression that thought and care has gone into the hallway, which makes for a great

Regardless of the size or constraint, a good hallway should have:

- A mirror to make the space look bigger.
- A console table or wall shelf for keys and post.
- A few coat hooks for everyday coats
- A bit of your personality – this could be a picture, a light fitting, a wall colour or a funky floor tile.

first impression. You can be quite dramatic with the lighting, using it to tell you where to go, or what door to go through. Wall lights work brilliantly in hallways because they give a quality of light that tends to soften the space, and you can use these low on the wall or high up to highlight changes in level or in height. Lighting at low level can be particularly effective as it will pool light on the floor to show you where to go, which creates focus on the floor and distracts you from the fact that the space may be small or dark.

Something I try to do on almost every project is to give the hallway a direct view to the back of the house. This means when you enter the hallway, you get a long view to somewhere else. It's not always possible but, when done correctly, it can open up vistas and visually connect spaces. I have incorporated countless large sliding doors into my designs – I say doors but they are more like walls, which are open 99 per cent of the time and only closed last thing at night – and using these means you can really connect the entrance hallway to the back of the house, something that not only works from a practical point of view but also makes everything look and feel bigger.

Another way of achieving this is to absorb the hallway into another room. Be careful with this because it depends on the function of that room. If there is a smaller room to the front of the house, perhaps used as a cloakroom, you could open this into the hallway and form a small seated area with organised storage for all the bits and bobs that are needed. This opens up the hallway and allows more light to come in, but still gives you the benefit of the storage that is needed. It's a great idea as long as the other spaces in the house are enough for your day-to-day living. Don't forget, context is king!

There are times when if you are stuck for space, it can be effective to get rid of a small hallway altogether and just have the entrance open into

> "It can be effective to get rid of a hallway altogether and just have the entrance open into the front room."

a front room, especially if you have the potential to build a porch to the front of the house. It may seem a bit odd, but when opening up existing houses with smaller hallways, if you incorporate the hallway into the front room, then all of a sudden you enter into a large hallway-cum-living room. You can use bookcases or low-level walls to break up the spaces a little if needed, but the overall aim here is to create the illusion of space as soon as you enter, which is especially effective if you have a tiny hallway. Done right, this can be really special, and all you had to do was knock down a wall! So simple, and yet so dramatic.

Design: Wesley O'Brien Design; Image: Barbara Egan

Sometimes, if the layout can accommodate it, you can move the entrance completely. I only ever do this when it is obviously in the wrong place and the infrastructure of the existing house is obviously incorrect, but it can make rooms bigger, streamline your long, narrow hallway and make the whole bones of the house function better. It's not always possible, but it's always worth considering because the knock-on effects can result in a dramatic transformation.

Removing one wall in the hallway solves two problems here. It makes a small hallway bright and open, and it makes a small front room feel bigger. The change in floor level still marks each zone, but the feeling of openness that this gives is a nifty trick if you are dealing with small spaces.

STAIRWAYS

If you're lucky enough to have a staircase, then you should make the most of it. If you're struggling with a staircase from a function point of view – maybe it interrupts a room upstairs or maybe it comes out in the wrong place – it is entirely possible that it *is* in the wrong place or is the wrong shape. It is possible to change the orientation or position of a staircase if necessary, which because it is an integral part of the infrastructure of the house, changes everything. It's major surgery but it reaps major benefits.

Sometimes, it can be the secret to fixing a lot of other problem areas in a house, so it needs a forensic eye to diagnose its condition and level of appropriateness. If space is tight, a spiral staircase can be a very efficient way of getting upstairs as they are light, delicate and

(Left) Design: Kingston Lafferty Design; Image: Donal Murphy Photography;
(Right) Design: De Siún Scullion Architects; Image: Paul Tierney Photography

Staircases can be features in
a room. Glass balustrades can
let light into dark staircases, or
a spiral staircase can add
character while saving space.
Every staircase is an opportunity
to get the design juices flowing.

Design: Kingston Lafferty Design; Image: Donal Murphy Photography

Metal handrails can bring a slightly edgier feel to a home. We are so accustomed to timber handrails, but introducing something more industrial can breathe new life into a tired staircase.

their footprint is minimal. It's not always practical, but sometimes it may be necessary depending on the project and the context. I've seen some amazing cottages in Ireland where the owners have implemented small spiral or metal staircases that were quite ingenious. The alternative would have been to install a much more clunky staircase, with a bigger footprint that would have adversely impacted on the rooms on both levels.

Staircases also offer up other opportunities. There is sometimes space under the stairs that can be ideal for a small toilet for guests, for utility storage off an entrance hallway, for kitchen storage, an office area or simply be left open to give a sense of space and openness. Staircases are a real joy to design as their potential is huge and there is no shortage of ideas about how to make the most of them – they are not just for getting upstairs.

If you have inherited a staircase in your home, chances are it is made of timber. These can look great if they are just sanded and painted, and left exposed without carpet. That would make them a bit noisier, but that doesn't bother some people, myself included. I like the echoing sound of people going up and down timber stairs – it must remind me of something.

Handrails and banisters can also look great with a lick of paint. Staining the handrail a dark glossy colour can really elevate a tired staircase, and give it a luxury hit as you run your hand along it. More modern staircases can be built from concrete, steel and other metals. This gives you more design options in term of finish and structure, and so can become expensive items in their own right. You can open the treads so the staircase looks lighter, and you can have seamless glass balustrades that can help keep a small space visually clutter free. Sometimes a space demands a staircase to match.

LANDINGS

In older houses, I always see wasted space at the top of a staircase.

An old tutor of mine used to say that after climbing a set of stairs, you should be rewarded. This could be in the form of a window, or maybe a bookcase with a small seat beside it. It could even be a beautiful light fitting or a painting that means something to you. Either way, when you get to the top of a staircase there should be something there for you – not a blank wall. This little trick has always stayed with me. I always try to get something into a landing – it could be a window, a chair, a small

At the top of this staircase, you are greeted (and rewarded) with an abundance of natural light and interesting views in every direction. Clever design, and beautiful detailing.

bookcase or a cool lamp, but give something to the arrival at the upper level.

If you have a window there, even better. If you are significantly redesigning your home, give plenty of thought to how you arrive at first-floor level. Hallways, staircases and landings should be thought of as more than just in-between spaces. They should embody the same character as the rest of the house, and a well-positioned chair can quickly become something you really come to appreciate and enjoy.

Just a little extra space here will go such a long way because we are generally used to dark, cramped corridors and staircases. Open them up a little, and use them for more than just passing through.

CORRIDORS

We've all been in dark corridors before, and they're not pleasant places to be. Generally, they're leading away from a hallway, or a staircase, to a series of bedrooms, or even to the main living areas in the house. Because the actual space of a corridor is nothing special, everything else needs to compensate. The space will not be forgiving, so you have to react.

We all know what these corridors look and feel like, so there are a few things to keep in mind. If you have to have a narrow space that leads to a couple of rooms, then think about the artificial lighting. Recessing light fittings and utilising LED strip lights are great ways to give a more sophisticated level of light instead of a standard downlight.

Design: Amanda Bone Architects; Image: Ros Kavanagh Photographer

Such a simple hallway, filled with light and interesting views upwards. Not very big, but it doesn't have to be and it still has something to offer.

I love the striped effect the natural light plays along this hallway wall, along with the big wall feature at the end. Goes to show that darkness can also be embraced in a hallway.

As corridors are usually smaller spaces, and because you pass through them, there is an opportunity to be a bit braver and introduce colours or textures that wouldn't work in a room where you spend longer periods of time. This means you can use a glossy paint finish on a wall to give it some depth, or can use a bright, bold colour to give an intense flash and some added energy to a dull space. Painting door architraves, doors and walls the same colour is a bit of a trend at the moment, but in a small, tight corridor space it really makes sense because your eye won't be interrupted by reading three separate colours or finishes. They will blend as one, and give the perception of the space being bigger. If you have a small, narrow corridor, my advice is to tackle the lighting head on, and be brave with the wall, ceiling and floor finishes.

"There is a saying that no matter what the design challenge is, nature has the answer."

There are lots of ways of connecting spaces, if that is what is intended. This can also include how we connect to our environment, from outside to inside. The notion of approach, entering and connecting is a fundamental part of how we read and interpret buildings, and a lot of it is rooted in our natural environment. In the design world, there is a saying that no matter what the design challenge is, nature has the answer. Millions of years of evolution has produced breathtaking beauty and pure function hand in hand in the natural world. We long to be connected to it, visually and physically. If you haven't got a window, get plenty of big green indoor plants in there. You really can't beat this in any room, not just the hallway.

THRESHOLDS

Blurring the boundaries between inside and outside is something we have heard a lot about in the past few years, and I think we are beginning to realise that opening up a large glass sliding door and stepping directly onto a patio area is generally a good feeling, and it works really well. This is what I mean by a threshold: what happens at that moment when inside becomes outside.

If you can keep the floor finish level inside and out, preferably using a similar flooring material, then you get a real sense of bringing the outside in, and the whole space will feel larger. Glass doors can now pull away to expose floating corners to further push this play on where the inside stops and the outside starts. We live in a temperate climate, and although we are not guaranteed long, lazy, warm sunny days end on end, we do have temperatures that are suitable for a better connection with the outdoors – even if you are in a woolly jumper. It doesn't have to be 26 degrees to sit outside.

Connecting with nature in the buildings and homes we design is something we all strive for. We all want to bring the outdoors into our living rooms, and it is easy to see why.

Design./Image: © Ebony and Co

Design: Dean Cooper & Co Image: Infinity Media

VOGUE COVERS

live

I've called this section live, because I can't think of a better way of describing everything that can happen in the room we are going to look at.

It has been called many things in the past – the lounge, the drawing room, the good room, the front room, the TV room, my gran called it the parlour – but, whatever it is, you need to think about what happens in it, so you can put together the right living room for you. If you're not happy with the feeling in your living room, ask yourself what it is that bothers you. Is it clutter? Is it space? Is it that the television dominates the room? Or some corner of the room is under-utilised? Is it the lighting? Is the furniture the correct scale, size and style? Is it comfortable? Is it in the wrong part of the house? Should it be moved to another room? Try and be as exact as you can, and think through all your options.

When you're not eating, sleeping, or bathing … then you're living, and you're probably doing it in this room. However, this can mean very different things to different people, so I always try to ensure that as many of these other activities are spread out across the house as possible, enabling a multitude of users and combinations and spaces to do different things. Everybody eats, bathes and sleeps, but we fill the rest of our days in different ways, so the more spaces we have available to us to read, watch television, listen to music, chat, snooze or tackle sudoku, the better placed our homes will be to keep everyone in them happy.

"The separate 'good room' has all but vanished."

A good question to ask yourself is: What rooms do you spend the most time in? Because changing these can have a huge effect on our quality of life. Even moving the television or placing a comfortable seat beside a window can change the way we spend our leisure time. If you feel like you spend too much time watching television, the answer may be to move the television so it doesn't dominate the room – or move it to a different room altogether.

It's amazing to think of the changes our homes have undergone in the past twenty years or so. The separate 'good room' has all but vanished, the back of the house is now where all the action is at and the front rooms can often be a little less loved. I know that's a bit of a sweeping statement, but I see it a lot – even in smaller houses.

The kitchen, usually at the back of the house, has undergone a huge transformation in recent years, becoming the centre of the house where the conversations happen and the kids do their homework. Of course, the kitchen has always been at the centre of the house, but our demands on it have changed. From being more private and modest spaces to the rear, we now want our kitchen to be a multifunctional space. The change in this thinking serves to illustrate how we, along with the needs of our homes, have changed in a relatively short period of time. It will take some time for many of the buildings we call home to catch up to this way of living, so we usually have to adapt what we have to create something for ourselves that is much more conducive to how we want and need to live.

Within your home, you will have to carve out a little corner for you to do whatever it is that you enjoy most in life. The living room can be a separate room or it can be part of an open-plan space. It can be a more private television room for example, or it can be a room that forms part of a bigger space for entertaining when dinner is finished. Before you start work on your home, have a good think about the following.

ORIENTATION

This has already been covered but it's so important, it's worth mentioning twice! If you are not undertaking a huge project where you are redesigning the entire house, you might think about improving the function and layout of your existing house by concentrating on the

Living rooms are about comfort. Cosy rugs and soft sofas are the obvious players in the perfect living room arrangement.

orientation of its rooms. If the sunniest side of the house is at the front, how can you make sure you are making the most of it? Can you create a semi-private garden at the front that feels like the back of the house? Can you move the kitchen to the front of the house so that it benefits from the morning light, and means the more evening-based rooms can go at the back? It's not possible to change the physical orientation of a house, but you can change the function of its rooms to make the most of the orientation you have. So don't be afraid to look at moving rooms from front to back or from downstairs to upstairs.

Design: Kingston Lafferty Design;
Image: Donal Murphy Photography

LAYOUT

As always, everything starts with the layout of your room.

Examine the shape of the room you have. Is it square or rectangular? Where are the doors in and out of the room, and are the windows sufficient? The amount and size of furniture should correspond to the shape and size of the room. This is something I see done incorrectly all the time, as people try to fit too much into a small room, or put furniture in the wrong place.

Draw out the room to scale and start to play with size of furniture and where to put what. Look at access into the room and see if that forces your hand in terms of how you can arrange things or whether changing this could open things up more.

Make a call early on in terms of how much furniture will fit in the room and what size it should be based on what you need. Can a small three-seater sofa and armchair and coffee table all fit in comfortably? Is that enough seating? People like to sit at angles to each other, and we generally congregate around a focal point. This harks back to the days of sitting around a fire, giving an open arrangement for communication and interaction. Armchairs and smaller sofas are good for arranging around a central table and, if you get the layout right, they should never have to move around and people shouldn't bump into them. If they do, the layout is wrong!

Design: ODKM Architects; Image: Infinity Media

Key elements to remember are:

- Keep furniture to scale in the room – if it's a small living room, maybe two big comfy chairs is all it can take.

- Don't clutter – less is more.

- Understand how the door opening and flow will affect your layout – can you change it?

- Establish your focus in the room; this is usually the television, the fireplace or a nice view!

- Fill in dead space with storage, bookcases or stand-alone pieces.

- Imagine sitting and using the room.

- Don't cram too much in. I would always rather have a limited amount of seating sitting comfortably in a space than too much furniture drowning the space. If you have a tiny living room, just run with it and make it comfortable – be ruthless with what goes into it.

FLOW

How we negotiate our way around items of furniture and between rooms should always be absolutely effortless and without obstruction or sudden jerky movements – and certainly without moving furniture around. This is generally called the flow, and it's extremely important in designing successful spaces. Problem rooms, or connecting spaces that don't work, are often the victims of poor or unresolved issues regarding the flow between and around them. If a door opens into a room and leads to another door, then this whole route has to be free from furniture, which dictates where pieces of furniture can go and, in turn, how you will light the room and how it will be used. If the space is large enough, you can interrupt this route with a table or a seating area, but the rule is that you must be able to comfortably flow around the object, like a running river flowing around a stone. Before you look at buying a sofa, the layout and flow of the room need to be established.

FOCUS

Whatever vibe you are going for in a living space, there is always a focus, and you will need to decide early on what this will be. The usual suspects are the television, the fireplace or a view. These need not be mutually exclusive, they can all exist together in harmony, but there should be a dominance of one over the other. The reason this is important is that it will influence the furniture, lighting and flow through a room … and you don't want to get any of that wrong.

Design: Martins Camisuli Architects; Image: Jake Fitzjones Photography

Great living spaces have everything in the right place, with a simple layout and comfortable furniture. If the TV is going to take centre stage, then you have to go for it. Here, it is balanced by the bookshelves and large windows.

Television

I love television. There is nothing I love more than sitting down and watching a really good film, scrunched up on a cosy sofa, shoes off, woolly socks on. But, in saying that, when I come home from work, I don't come into the room and switch it on automatically and leave it on all evening. Let's be honest, there is a lot of rubbish on! Your TV shouldn't be a distraction, especially when it's off.

The television should never be the focus of a living room, and while we may watch television in this room, it shouldn't dominate the space. In saying this, if the living room is the main television room and TV is your thing, then you want to ensure that you can slouch all over the sofa and that the room is primed for watching it – it's a difficult balancing act.

Design: Plus Architecture; Image: Donal Murphy Photography

I would very rarely put a television high up on a wall, in fact I have done it just once on the demands of the client. It can work in certain instances, but you will be making a big impact on a space by doing this, and I think the main television focus is best done in a separate room if you can. Try and conceal the television behind sliding storage doors, so you can close it off if needed. Alternatively, if you have it off to one side of, say, the fireplace, then even though it is in the room, the fireplace is still in charge of the space.

The proof they say is in the pudding. I visit good friends of mine all the time; they have two kids and they have a lovely small extension to the back of their house that connects to the garden. It contains a small kitchen, dining table, facing sofas beside large bi-folding doors, an easy chair and a stereo. Everything happens in this room and, to this day, we still never really use the television room which is at the front of the house. This arrangement works because they have that separate room that can specifically house the television and be set up for that alone. When I am over, we are all of us (kids as well) in the back of the house, and the quality of enjoying each other's company, talking and playing with the kids is all the more potent for the lack

of a television in this space. This is the reason that I generally put the main television somewhere else if possible – it frees up these spaces to be so much more.

If you have the space to allocate a room to be a dedicated television room, then, of course, it takes centre stage, and the challenge is to create a dedicated room with prime focus on watching television. These can look really luxurious and it's essentially just a room with an obvious prime focus on a television, along with a cosy sofa and maybe some carpet. Again, the question is whether you feel this kind of dedication is right for you, and whether the other spaces in the house can enable it. If you only have one open-plan space that has to contain the living room, then you should think carefully about where you place the television and how much impact you want it to have.

I always feel that a living room is about relaxing when the dinner is done, or the kids are in bed, or you come back from work late. If that's what it's really about, then there is nothing more peaceful, relaxing or welcoming than a roaring fire.

Fire

If you can get both, then a nice fire alongside the television can work great. Just keep in mind the size and proportion that will best fit the room. The light and heat of a natural flame can dance around a room and give you the comforting warmth that

feels so good on a cold November evening. That, coupled with a cup of tea and your favourite television programme – happy days.

There are all sorts of fires that are right for different reasons – open fires, gas fires, solid fuel stoves – and each looks and feels different. Bear in mind that if the fire is to be the focus of the room, how it is dressed will also have a big impact. A gas fire, for example, is usually built in and plastered into the wall, so the size of the opening can be quite modest in comparison to the large Victorian fireplaces that made them an area of focus in the first place. For this reason, you will need to think about how the fire itself will work with its surrounds.

You will need a hearth to absorb the heat and, in small spaces, it is great if you can get this flush with the floor finish – which will also remove a trip hazard. No matter how small, I always try and keep the use of a fireplace wherever possible. I have kept them in bathrooms and dressing rooms, and while they may be used rarely, they still give you the option of bringing the life, character and sometimes smell into rooms every now and again and, let's be honest, who wouldn't love a bath beside an open fire!

The view

We all love to sit beside a window or to look out on a nice view, but we shouldn't necessarily direct all our furniture towards it.

In a living room, there are other activities that need to be catered for and, most of the time, people don't sit on a sofa and stare intently out the window, so it works better in the peripheral. Directing a main couch towards a window would also mean that, from other areas in the room, we would have to look at the back of a sofa, and this would interrupt the flow of a room. Unless you're lucky enough to have the space for several couches or chairs, in which case one could be positioned towards the view – but, for the most part, it doesn't make sense to point a sofa towards a window. In addition, as living rooms are generally used more in the evening, orientating towards the view may not be the best idea as it could glare, though this does depend on the aspect of the room.

Of course, the view is always there and is always something we are aware of. It's about trying to get the other things happening in the space to work without compromising the view – that is the actual challenge of making your living room work if you're lucky enough to have a nice view.

I love bench seats and window seats, as these make you feel like you're really close

Great big comfy corner sofa orientated invitingly towards the room. This shouldn't be misconstrued as ignoring the fabulous view – trust me, you will still appreciate the view with this layout.

to the outdoors. If you have a small area of dead space in a room, ask yourself if it is a space where you could add in something like this. A bench can offer seating, but also extra storage which can come in handy. These seats can sometimes become the best seat in the house so they're a great example of clever design really giving you something back in return.

Entertaining in our homes is something we all love to do. A small bar or drinks cabinet, and a decent music setup are great additions to any space to easily engage party mode.

Design: Plus Architecture; Image: Donal Murphy Photography

PARTY TIME

I am a musician as well as an architect, in fact I was on a career path to play flute professionally until I had a change of heart and went into architecture. Despite this career change, my love for music has never diminished, and I listen to everything from classical to techno, depending on the mood I am in or what task I am doing. Music is just such a great mood setter, and if you need to get the party started then nothing else will do.

Have a think about where you might have your music setup – this can be just a couple of speakers adjacent to a working area or a dedicated sideboard with speakers and a music system. I have a setup with my turntable and decks (I also DJ) and speakers all on top of an old sideboard with the speakers at each end. I can always plug in my laptop and play anything online, so I know if I need good music, I have it all set up and ready to go … and it gets used all the time.

If you are doing extensive work on your house, you could have built-in speakers installed in the ceilings or walls that are connected back to an electronic panel on a wall – which I am sure you can imagine is quite something when throwing parties or relaxing on a Sunday afternoon. If you are an audiophile, give this some thought. It doesn't need to be fancy, just get a system setup that suits you. Music is medicine, after all.

Bar

Depending on how much you entertain, there is nothing more decadent than a small bar if you have the space for it. Usually this can be concealed behind a set of retractable doors, and if you are doing a large amount of work, then it may be something that is worth thinking about. We have designed a couple of bars and they're really practical and fun.

All that's needed is a small sink and some storage. You can add in a small refrigerator if you want to go all the way but as long as you have something there for entertaining, you will definitely use it. I have a solid silver tray with a few bottles of fine whiskey on it – not much, but it's something!

RESTING

Resting is not solely for the bedroom. Resting is not sleeping, it is just being at ease, and comfort plays a huge part in this. It is strongly linked with meditation and reflection and, in the age of the digital revolution where we are bombarded and saturated with information and data on a constant basis, the need to rest has never been more important, for our health if nothing else.

Think about what puts you at ease, and what you enjoy doing. If you enjoy reading, then something as simple as an appropriately positioned comfortable chair and a good light can be all you need to really give that activity a good home. Maybe this can be beside a built-in floor-to-ceiling bookcase, so you have a corner nook with a great big love chair to curl up in with a good book.

I always find that when you have spaces that are set up for certain activities, then you will find them being used, which means you are doing more of what you love to do. The same goes for listening to music or sewing or whatever. Think about what you would like to do and then make a home for it. It doesn't have to be anything special, but at least you're filling your home with spaces that are *your* kind of spaces.

The holy trinity of good living

The most important piece in the living-room jigsaw is the sofa. The best piece of general advice I've been given about living was to make sure you have a good bed, a good shower, and a good sofa – they are the holy trinity of good living. I think the reason this rings so true is that they all hit a reset button inside us, and we can take a minute to let the day wash over us, as we retreat into ourselves.

Choosing a sofa is not an easy decision to make, so you have to revert to the practicalities of what you need, along with the context for your life, and then make your decision. If you have four kids, the delicate cream velvet sofa that you fell in love with is probably not the best choice, you may need to go with leather for ease of cleaning – at least until they get older. My sisters both have leather sofas and I am sure they are thankful for them every time they clean up the spillages, which seems to be a daily occurrence. My nieces and nephews try to kill those sofas every day, and, though they get close, they fail! Leather is the perfect choice if you have young kids as it is really durable and wipe clean and yet retains a sense of design style and luxury that is great for after they potter off to bed and the adults can play.

I think as soon as you start worrying about damage or usability of anything, then the things you own end up owning you. Furniture is there to be used and abused, so choose wisely. If it's well made and it fits in with your lifestyle, then it should stand the test of time.

Sofas have to be versatile. They have to work aesthetically yet be equally at home providing optimum comfort for an all-day box set binge. They may also need to be a bed, a trampoline or a dinner table, so it's a tough gig for a sofa.

I always put comfort at the very top of the list, and everything else can follow. At the end of the day, if I'm not comfortable, then nothing else matters, which is why I go on and on about comfort being at the very epicentre of what good design is. You should be able to keep your feet on the ground and recline fully back to the cushion supports. Armrests on sofas are great, as is a mid-sized back. A lower-back sofa can look great until you try and watch that boxset, and you suddenly realise that the clean lines and streamlined structured finish is not overly suited to lengthy periods of sofa surfing.

In choosing a sofa, regardless of material or shape, you should always look for quality. This doesn't mean expensive, just evaluate the quality of the construction materials. The best kinds are made of a solid metal or hardwood frame, with spring or foam support. After this, it's all about the quality of the fabric and padding, so don't be afraid to jump onto the sofa in a showroom and get into it properly to evaluate its comfort levels. If it ain't comfy, don't buy it!

Also, I wouldn't advise buying a three-piece suite (sofa and two armchairs) unless you have quite a grand living space that can comfortably take the size and the continuity. Most living rooms that I see, even in quite grand homes, still can't really carry it off properly. It's also quite a traditional thing to do, which is why they always looks great in a period mansion house, but we don't live in huge, period mansion houses and I think there is far more interest in mixing and matching furniture.

Mixing and matching also means that you are not tied to one finish across the entire furniture in a room, which will help prevent the need to replace it all at the same time. If you mix it up, you can add pieces and replace pieces more easily, which

"The best piece of general advice I've been given about living was to make sure you have a good bed, a good shower, and a good sofa."

Design: ODKM Architects; Image: Sasfi Hope Ross

This is a take on a 'conversation pit' – where the seating is built in and angled in such a way as to promote good chat. What you can't see is the TV, which is hidden behind the sliding timber screen so as not to dominate the room.

This minimal workstation is perfect for the owner because it avails of the bright natural light and height in the room, so it is a nice place to sit, but it can also be easily folded away when not needed. Great flexibility.

Design: Maxime Laroussi/Urban Agency; image: Barbara Egan

will keep things fresh. You can also pair a cool armchair with quite a simple sofa, giving a variety of seating types; this is a cost-effective way to keep hold of an old piece to make it work in a bigger ensemble.

TV dinners are great – I won't lie, they're a regular enough occurrence in my life. I don't have kids and can work all hours through the week, so every now and again we hit the sofa to eat and collapse after a long day, and I know a lot of people are the same. It doesn't happen every day but, when it does, I make sure we have the right setup. It's all about the furniture. A low-level table for setting down plates and higher-level table for the rest, mainly cups of tea or a glass of wine. This means that we don't have to balance our plates on our knees and the glass of wine has its home far away from the fabric of the grey sofa. Simple things really, but life-changing if you do this regularly. It's always the smallest of changes that can have the biggest impact.

WORKING

Certain jobs and lifestyles lend themselves to working from home. You will need to have a dedicated area or room for this, but in fact most households today would benefit from a well-designed corner from which to do the household paperwork.

Because of the internet and wireless technology, our homes have never before been so well set up for working from home, but certain things need to be considered to make sure your working life doesn't overspill and contaminate other spaces in your home! You don't need a lot to create a great working space, indeed the mantra 'small is beautiful' has never been more apt.

The first thing to establish is what you need. How often do you work from home? Once a week? Once a month? Regularly? The answer to this will dictate the size and design of your workstation.

As a minimum, I would always have a small office chair, concealed storage and some form of desk located somewhere in the house. This can be small, but you may be surprised how often it is used. I have it in my own home and I am writing from it now.

The ideal solution is a separate room, a fully fitted home office, if you work from home regularly. This doesn't have to be big but, if it is a big part of your life, then this is what you should aim for. It gives privacy and helps keep a degree of separation (albeit psychological) between your work and the rest of your life.

The workstation can be hidden behind a large, sliding, bi-folding door, so it can open into the room when needed, but be completely closed off when not. If you haven't got a separate room, other spaces in the house can be utilised as a work area – maybe in an attic space, a spare bedroom or in a quiet separate dining room. These can work very well, especially if you don't work from home every day, as they are, in a sense, concealed – however, covered storage will be key in enabling the space to still operate as it was originally intended without the feeling of there being an office in the way.

If you don't have the luxury of a separate room, integrating a working space into the everyday spaces of a house, such as a kitchen or a living room, is often the only viable solution and can work really well. The flexibility of the space will depend solely on how well-designed the room is. Again, concealed storage and clever retractable desktops will be fundamental in ensuring you can set it up for working when needed – and equally get rid of it when the kids come back from school or you have people over for dinner.

> "The ideal solution is a separate room, fully fitted home office, if you work from home regularly."

(Top) Design: Kingston Lafferty Design; Image: Donal Murphy Photography; (Bottom) Design/Image: Dulux (Nutmeg White)

Hardware

Some of the plug-in items, like printers and scanners, can still be rather unsightly and you should conceal them. You may also have to maintain a hardwire connection to a laptop or desktop computer. Cables and large, clunky devices are things that you definitely want out of sight, especially if this is in a shared space in the house, so think about where they're going to be housed and then it's a case of damage limitation.

Built-in units are great for housing these big items, and you can design retractable or fold-away doors to conceal them when not in use. Maybe the storage unit can be closed from one side but open from another so it is concealed from general view. The key here is to think about these big items before you start, and then decide how best to deal with them. A simple shelf may be all that is required.

Storage

Storage is so important in a working space. And, of course, what we mean is 'closed' storage, unless you are happy to have messy work on show 24/7. Keep it simple, drawers, shelves and cupboards will all get used, so figure out where your working space will be, how big it will be, and the minimum amount of storage you will need – and stick to it!

Lighting

Natural light is the best feature in any room and your workspace should be no different. We all want to sit beside a window, but more often than not these little working zones are tucked away in a dark corner somewhere. If possible, get it beside a window. Optimum light and fresh air are the natural stimulants for productive minds.

For burning the midnight oil, all you really need is a good-quality desk light. An angle-poise light is the designer's choice because of its classic lines and flexibility for moving around and shining light onto different areas. Anything else is overkill.

The key to all of this is to really think about how you work, and whether you need to integrate a space like this into your home. The answer is different for everyone, so only you know what your needs are.

All work and no play …

PLAYING

When I talk about a play space, I don't necessarily mean just for kids, and I definitely don't mean a separate room for it. I get a lot of clients coming to me wanting a playroom – a separate room, adjacent to the kitchen or living room, so that the kids can be separated, but still watched over. In my experience, this doesn't work. I think the issue is really about storage – a need for somewhere to put bikes and buggies, and occasionally to keep the noise in! And the answer is not a playroom, it is for a multifunctioning space that kids can own during the day but that can become an adult space at night. This is the real design brief, and is how this issue should be addressed as it also future proofs your home design.

A separate playroom can quickly become a storage room that can quickly become an underused storage wasteland. I've seen this in so many houses, where the playroom is located at the front of the house. It's never used, and it becomes a problem. This, then, feeds into a need to 'extend' as there is not enough usable space, but the answer is sometimes straight in front of you. These redundant playrooms need to be reintegrated into our living spaces, and it is through design that we can get them to be flexible and multifunctional, suitable for the kids during the day and the adults at night.

Design: Kingston Lafferty Design; Image: Donal Murphy Photography

Good storage choices will make any room in the house function better. They also enable spaces to be flexible – these spaces can have one function during the day, and quickly change their tone later at night.

Storage

In order for a space to be multifunctional, storage is key, so that the room can take on different personalities at different times of the day. When the paint and colouring and jigsaws and homework is done, you need good storage to clear everything away and assume the grown-up mode in the room. You may want to keep some toys or pictures on display, so think about your storage options when deciding on how polarising you want the spaces to be.

If I have one common request from every client, it is for more storage. We cannot get enough of it. We are all hoarders at heart, and while there is a healthy balance to this, there is no doubting the sheer mass of stuff we accumulate over time, never mind when we start sharing spaces with others or start a family.

Space is at a premium in every home, big or small, and ensuring you have adequate and well-thought-out storage can often be the key to making successful spaces work. It may not take all the glory, but it plays a key supporting role without which most houses just simply wouldn't work. So here is how to get it right.

This sounds obvious, but most rooms need a bit of storage in one form or another. It can be a utility room that needs a lot, or just a simple sideboard in a living room – but whatever it is, only put in it things that you need, and think about how much storage you require in any particular space from the very start. My number one piece of advice for people who think they don't have enough storage is to throw out more stuff. Most people can regain 20–30 per cent of their storage space by carrying out a good spring clean. You should know what's in your storage areas, they shouldn't be a forgotten wasteland – if they are, you are definitely overdue a clean-up.

Open and closed

Storage means everything from the golf bag that is used once a year to the priceless vase you want displayed in a room. There are lots of

Big or small, house or apartment living, you should have a living room that has:

A good focal point:
Fireplace, television, view – it's up to you!

Good lighting:
We don't need to oversaturate living rooms with light. Keep it dark and moody with task lighting, and keep the ambient lighting to low-level wall lights.

A comfy sofa, and armchair if possible:
This is heaven at the end of a long, hard day.

Good flow:
Know the flow and don't mess with it.

Good layout:
Regardless of size, you need to nail this because it will affect how the space is used.

Design/Image: Dulux (Paint effect created with Flame Frenzy 5 & Chiffon White 4)

different types of storage, and you can describe them as either open or closed. Some items you want to see every day – books and CDs – you want them close at hand, instantly accessible, or you want them to hold and display items that have particular meaning to you. Others, you don't mind being stacked in behind a door for a while and forgotten about. A balance of both always works well, and the decision should be traced back to what you actually need.

Most of us don't want to live in a minimalist world with nothing of any real personal interest on show, but we also don't want to look at clutter every day. Think about what is going to be stored and how. Some items we will always want hidden, and some will look great on show and you will love having them part of the room. Think about it.

eat

Eating. It is one of life's greatest pleasures. The American modernist architect Frank Lloyd Wright put it well: 'Dining is, and always was, a great artistic opportunity.' I think what he means by this is that there is a difference between eating, cooking and dining – and I want to talk about all three.

Chances are that, like me, you have done it all – street food sitting on a kerb, fine dining, sofa dinners, hot dogs on the run, Sunday dinners, late-night takeaways, lazy brunches – you name it, we've all done it. There are many different environments for enjoying food, and each is perfect in its own way. We have an enduring, never-ending love affair with food in our homes, and we need to create the right kind of spaces to make our meal times – no matter what they are – enjoyable and comfortable. To do this, we need to make sure we have well-designed spots in our homes that can take the Christmas dinner for twelve, as well as the late-night guilty takeaway on the sofa on a Friday night.

There is a worry at the moment, which has been building in the past couple of decades, that the majority of families regularly have dinner watching television, or even dine in separate rooms, quickly and at different times. For me, the kitchen is the heart and soul of any home. It is where people gather and conversation happens. Memories are made at kitchen tables, and there is something intrinsically primal about gathering around a table to eat with the people closest to you. It's also the best way to teach kids table manners!

COOKING

Growing up, we always had a small table right inside the kitchen, so we were always on top of one another. It was mayhem when my mum was cooking, but it was all about the food and the chat. To this day, when I go home I go straight for the fridge, pull out some food, sit at the table and start talking. Actually, I do this in all of my friends' houses too! It's such a comforting thing; I feel secure, safe and at home when I sit at a table. Funnily enough, at home, there is always someone in the kitchen as well. My family home, even today, is still not a three-meals-a-day place; it never stops, and that's why although it is a cliché, the kitchen really is the heart of the home.

The kitchen is so often the main area for redesign in any project. We are a nation obsessed with our kitchens, but I suppose we always have been. They can be large and showy for the exhibitionist chef, or small and a little cramped in smaller houses and apartments. They can be rooms in themselves or part of an open-plan

Kitchen style is something I feel we are much more familiar with. I think deep down, we all know what kind of kitchen we really want.

(Left) Design: Kingston Lafferty Design; Image: Donal Murphy Photography;
(Right) Design/Image: Porter & Jones Kitchen

arrangement with the dining room, and maybe even have a lounge space with couches or armchairs, which is great if you have the space for it. They can be free-standing or built in, and range in styles from the country classic to the ultra modern. But no matter what type of kitchen you have, cooking a meal for someone and enjoying it in their company is good for your soul – so forget about the showy side of things and get right down to how you want to cook.

As for any design task, your kitchen starts with you. How do you like to cook? Do you cook at all? Do you like to talk to others while cooking or do you like to be semi-hidden away somewhere in case you burn the spuds? We're all different, so you need to find the chef in you and then give them what they need. Maybe you love to cook outside, if so, you could think about a space for that too. As always, start with the big questions.

Orientation

Kitchens are best placed near as much natural light as you can get – this is because we demand so much more from our kitchens today and spend so much more time in them. East-facing spaces are great for capturing the morning sunlight. If they connect to a south- or west-facing dining space then, in the evening, you will still have the last remnants of sunshine coming into the room, so we always orientate these spaces in this way where possible. If you subscribe to the open-kitchen-dining

Design: Plus Architecture; Image: Donal Murphy Photography

social space and currently find these spaces located to the north and want to bring in more light, then you may want to consider moving your kitchen entirely to a sunnier part of the house, or opening through to a room to borrow some sunlight.

You can also get more light by having taller windows. Make more of them, run them right up to the ceiling, introduce new floor-to-ceiling glazing along a wall or, if you are extending, increase the ceiling height in the space to allow in more diffuse light from longer windows. You may even be able to introduce a roof light to capture east- or west-facing light, so you can pull light into a north-facing back kitchen area.

Layout

The auld triangle – not the song, but the tried and tested optimum working arrangement in any kitchen. This is rooted in pure function and usability, and has stood the test of time. It is one of those rules that shouldn't be broken (if you can help it). It is effectively triangulating a space that is marked by the sink, the fridge and the cooker, enabling ease of unobstructed access to each. Of course, it is not always possible given room layouts and constraints – and sometimes personal preference. As long as you keep this function in mind, then you can alter it a little if you need to.

(Top) Design: ODKM Architects; Image: Barbara Egan; (Bottom left) Design: NOJI Architects; Image: Alice Clancy Photography; (Bottom right) © ariadna de raadt/Shutterstock.com

The size of your room, its proportions and the flow through the different spaces will dictate the layout most suitable for the room. The kitchen layout should directly correspond to the constraints it has to work within, so you should analyse the space and decide on the best layout that will fit the space.

I don't prescribe to the formal named layouts as pure design, but they're a good starting point to give you an idea of what layout is going to work best.

Galley

Galley kitchens are exactly what they sound like. They are long and linear, and usually used in tight spaces as they are a very efficient use of space. Try and go for more generous worktop depth (750 mm instead of the usual 600 mm) as this will take appliances more easily, and also gives you that extra worktop depth that is so useful in a tight spot. Try to incorporate a galley kitchen where you have space at either end for an island or a small table where people can keep you company as you cook.

Even if you don't have the space for a seated area to eat, a well-positioned window seat or bench or stool can give that feeling that someone else can chill in the kitchen while you cook – as opposed to them feeling like they are in the way all the time.

L-Shape

Again, this is exactly what it sounds like, where units run along perpendicular walls to give the optimum in working ergonomics. I like to do this with a run of wall units along one length and then have the other 'arm' work a bit like an island, jutting into the room if the space enables it. This can work very well, when they open onto an informal small dining space or in conjunction with a full island, which gives an even better arrangement of space for working and sitting down.

U-Shape

This is where the L-shape is completed, and will give the most amount of storage and worktop area. They can be a bit restrictive and clunky and can dominate a room. Of course, there will be times when it is necessary, so take heed of its size and visual weight in a space and try to keep it to a minimum.

Small spaces

I think it is worth talking about small spaces, indoors and outdoors, and making them work as kitchen and dining areas. Some of the best restaurants in NYC operate out of tiny kitchens with customers squeezed into even smaller spaces. They are a great example of how size doesn't matter when it comes to eating. The customers are happy and the food is good, all within tiny spaces – proving that it is possible to make small kitchens work to your advantage.

Making a good kitchen work does not need to be complicated. People often complain that they never have enough room in the kitchen. Below is a series of tips I've put together to help you deal with the most common issue I get asked about – lack of space. Extra storage can go a long way if there isn't a separate utility room, when the kitchen may also need to house the washing machine and the dryer. You can buy combined washer/dryers which are a handy way to reclaim storage space in a small kitchen. Space-saving is about utilising what you have, and also keeping the worktop as free from clutter as you can. This means utilising the walls and the storage available under units.

Open shelving:

In small spaces, keep shelving open and easy to hand. This will make the space seem bigger and also make it easier to use. There is no need to spend a lot on a fancy kitchen; simple open shelves with pots and pans everywhere can look great and function brilliantly. Throw in a few nice pots and pans and, before you know it, you have a designer look and not a cluttered mess. I would always recommend open storage at upper levels in smaller kitchens as closed storage will feel as if it is on top of you.

Quirky storage:

From magnet strips, to clip on items on exposed rails, there are many ways to keep knives and utensils easily available but not taking up valuable worktop space. You can even use these for other everyday items, such as salt, pepper, olive oil and spices – everything at hand, no opening and closing doors, no more Chinese Five Spice falling out on your worktop (guilty). Get clever with open storage to make a small kitchen function better, and therefore seem bigger.

Limited space:

With limited space, storage is obviously critical, but if you use wall-mounted units things can get a little on top of you. Instead, hang your collectables on the wall and even from the ceiling. Make sure to invest in a few nice pots and get a good mix of stuff all close to hand and ready to go. This is very practical and functional, and looks great.

Fridges:

Fridges are the biggest item in any kitchen, so an under-counter fridge is a great way to save space and free up worktop space. It also keeps you more in tune with its contents and less likely to forget about the carrot stuck at the back of one of the large storage bins (guilty again!).

Clean as you go:

This isn't really a design tip, it's just a simple fact of life. If you clean as you go, your kitchen will be bigger because your limited worktop space is free from obstructions. Wall-mounted drying racks are great for this.

(Top) © nomadFra / Shutterstock.com;
(Bottom) Design/Image: Dulux (Perfectly Greige)

If you are tight for space, no matter what, try to get a little table and chairs in and just go with it. Fold down tables and chairs are great to pull out when needed, and you can even look at wall-mounted tables that fold away when not in use. Regardless of how limiting space might be, carve out a place to sit for dinner.

If you have a shed or an outhouse in the back garden, or a garage that mostly holds junk, think about knocking through and utilising some of that space. Even if you can allocate the more utility items here, such as the washing machine or a walk-in larder, this will free up other areas in the kitchen and can make all the difference.

Kitchen features

Island

Having an island in a kitchen is probably the ideal for all of us, as it provides a good slab of worktop space that connects the kitchen to the surrounding space, which can be an informal dining spot like a breakfast bar, or indeed into an open dining space that is part of the kitchen itself. These things make it a wonderfully social and useful thing to have. You can also put a sink into an island, so their practicalities cannot be underestimated. It also gives set down space so if you entertain often, and need helping hands in the kitchen, or just like the company, then it provides a great, usable and practical space.

> "Having an island in a kitchen is probably the ideal for all of us."

I have designed islands that have wheels, which is a great way to give some flexibility to how you arrange your kitchen space. It can act as a movable worktop, a drinks trolley, or to serve or move things around when preparing, or it can be completely moved out of the way if you're having a party in the kitchen – and, as we all know, the kitchen is the best place to be at a party. As the island usually forms part of a bigger kitchen, it also provides an opportunity to play with the finish and do something different from that in the main body of the kitchen. You obviously need plenty of space to make an island work and enable ease of movement around it.

Appliances

Appliances can be a minefield, so I am going to keep my advice about them short and sweet. As always, understand your context – who you are and how you want to cook – as this will determine what appliances will suit you best. They can be quite varied, and can take on multiple functions, so it can be a bit daunting making the decision that best suits you.

Design/Image: ODKM Architects and Porter & Jones Kitchen

All you budding chefs, read on …

Gas hobs give you instant heat control, whereas electric hobs are either straightforward ceramic or induction – this has a built-in sensor that reacts when connected with the surface of the pot or pan, and they look quite slick, usually in black glass. Induction hobs require a magnetic connection with the surface of the pan so some pans may not work with them, which is one of the reasons I'm not so keen on them. I prefer gas because I find it is much easier to control the heat when I'm cooking.

Ovens have become so versatile, they can do a lot more than the standard grill and fan options. Combination steam and convection ovens are the newest types and offer all the health benefits of steam cooking (preserving more nutrients in the food) while also offering all the benefits of convection cooking. You can have single or double oven, depending on the demands of your kitchen, and there are also handy little shelf ovens that you can add in to your design if you want some extra space, but not a complete additional oven.

An oven can be built in, stacked on top of one another or under-counter – all personal preferences depending on the style of the kitchen. They say the ovens are better positioned at waist height for ease of extracting oversized Christmas turkeys, but if you are short (like me) then this kind of depends on your own height … so give it some thought.

Kitchen showrooms are amazing, they stock everything and they have specialist staff who can guide you in the right direction. So go along and ask lots of questions before you buy anything.

Kitchen design is like anything else – form has to follow function. Although incredibly stylish, this kitchen layout is remarkably simple, and has a couple of flourishes in the wall and floor finishes to give it a unique designer feel.

Materials

In choosing materials for your kitchen, remember it's all about the balance of character, functionality and cost that is the most suitable for you. These can sometimes be intertwined with style, but you can have a painted timber kitchen that is traditional or contemporary, and in some instances both.

As a general rule, I would always concentrate on the things you touch and feel, like the worktop, the door handles (if you have any) and the taps, because these are what really make a kitchen. A very simple carcass can be used and you would never really know the difference … unless you're that way inclined. I'm not!

Worktops

Worktops are all about functionality for me, and I would push the boat out as far as you can to get the best quality you can afford. They are prone to damage and take so much abuse during their lifespan, so this should really lead your decision making. In small kitchens, you can splurge a bit on worktops or splashbacks, as the areas you're dealing with aren't too large and therefore costs should be manageable. A good worktop is a good investment, but it need not cost the earth. Splashbacks are an opportunity for colour, creativity and to be a bit bold if you feel brave enough. Glazed tiles, back-painted glass or mosaic tiles, the options are endless and your creativity should have a good home here. If you want to change your kitchen but can't afford a

> "A good worktop is a good investment, but it need not cost the earth."

brand new one, sometimes all a kitchen needs is a new worktop and a coat of paint on the doors and this can transform what you already have. It just goes to show how important the visual and tactile elements are in the kitchen.

Ideally, I like to be able to put hot pans down anywhere on a worktop in case my cooking doesn't go exactly to plan and I have to freestyle at short notice, so I always aim for a non-porous durable material like stone. Bullet proof and beautiful, that's all I want in a worktop. Granite has been popular for ages and rightly so. The variety of

(Top left) Design: NOJI Architects; Image: Alice Clancy Photography; (Top right) Design/Image: Dulux (Apron Grey); (Bottom) Design: Kingston Lafferty Design; Image: Donal Murphy Photography

Function and style on show in the kitchen through simple design choices.

colours and textures, and its hardened properties, make it ideal. Slate can be very beautiful as well but may need to be oiled and maintained, so this is something you need to factor in. Certain stones also have to be sealed, and will be stained by acidic or citrus elements (like lemon juice), so it is always best to ask a specialist when you choose your worktop. I've also been impressed with quartz worktops because of their high level of durability and the choice of colour and texture available. These are man-made composite materials that can be every bit as beautiful as a natural stone finish.

I like a timber worktop for the softness and warmth that it can bring into a kitchen, something that can be lost with a contemporary design. They also require maintenance though, and often stain around the sink, so they need to be oiled regularly.

Just remember that it's all about how you want to live your life – that is the only real thing that you need to consider. If you are happy to be careful and maintain a softer worktop, then that is absolutely fine. If you have timber already in the room, on the floor or in the windows, then think about matching them – which can be difficult. That said, contrasting wood can be very beautiful, but it takes more skill as it is much harder to get right.

Corian worktops are quite amazing. I have loved Corian since I used it in designing the public sinks in a well-known British football stadium while working in London – that's how durable it is! It is composed of acrylic polymer and alumina trihydrate (ATH), a material derived from bauxite ore, and it has endless potential. It is non-porous and can be formed and moulded to give seamless sinks as part of the worktop, and it is extremely hygienic, durable and beautifully soft to touch.

It's heat resistance and fireproof properties enable it to withstand high temperatures, and I have seen demonstrations where they blowtorch it and it is unscathed. Its practicalities coupled with its beautiful soft touch make it a real favourite.

At the more cost-effective side of things, laminate can be used if you stick to simple block colours and don't try to mimic a stone material. Materials should look like what they are, otherwise it's just fake – so if you're going with a laminate worktop, be bold with it. I actually quite like stainless steel or metal worktops, even if they do scratch. They add an industrial feel to a kitchen and I quite like that because I do see the kitchen as a living and breathing place of industry. I don't mind the imperfections and the wear and tear, it's part of showing that the kitchen is used.

My least favourite finish for a worktop would be tiles or glass. These worktops are just not the most practical thing in the world, and I haven't seen one beautiful enough to convince me to overlook those impracticalities. Also, using sharp knives and banging pots around something delicate like glass just makes me wince a bit.

Whatever worktop you go for, always make sure you have big gnarly chopping boards, and lots of them. Good knives hate hard stone, so for all slicing, dicing, chopping and bashing, make sure to use nature's finest as your surface. Your knives will stay sharper for longer.

Cabinet doors

The doors of your kitchen cabinets will have the biggest impact on how your kitchen looks and feels, so there are a couple of options to consider. It's all in the detail, however, and you can play around with the rules.

Architects love plywood, and if you're on a budget this is not only cost-effective but will look terrific.

Solid timber is a classic choice and, in its natural state, will help give a more traditional feel. You can counter this by having a concealed or handle-less kitchen, which provides a nice mix of traditional in the material and contemporary in the finish. This also gives way to a slick and seamless door system which adds to the contemporary feel.

A painted timber-panelled door with a stainless steel handle can still give a contemporary look to your kitchen, but it is in the fine

detail that this will be won and lost. A contemporary colour with a contrasting work-top can provide all the luxury of a contemporary kitchen with the familiarity of a traditional echo.

A spray-painted finish is a more standardised timber door finish, and all you have to do is select a colour.

In terms of handles, you generally have something visible as an element in its own right, like a stainless steel handle or a funky knob, or you build them into the material itself. The most contemporary option is to hide them altogether with a handleless door, which gives that ultra-slick modernist aesthetic.

Again, there is no right or wrong answer here, it's all about finding out what is right for you. It might surprise you to know that my favourite kitchens are always those that have been kind of jumbled together. As an architect, I can, of course, appreciate the slick contemporary lines of the modern kitchen, but there is just a timeless charm to kitchens that are not pristine. I like to see kitchens that have evolved over a period of time.

If you can't do your kitchen all at once, then don't worry about it – do it bit by bit, the end result will still work just as well.

Ergonomics

As a rule, worktop units are approx. 900 mm high and island units around 100–150 mm higher. Walking between units (in a galley kitchen, for example), you should allow for around 1,200–1,500 mm, depending on constraints, and around a dining table always give as much room as possible, but at least 1 metre. Overhead units should be at least 500 mm above the worktop, and the extractor hood approx. 750 mm. Most kitchen units are 600 mm deep, but if you can extend this to 700 mm (or even a little more) it will make a real difference.

Lighting

The one room that demands good task lighting is the kitchen. In fact, it is the perfect room to illustrate the different types of lighting available as it requires all three – ambient, task and accent – you'll find that a kitchen–dining space that doesn't have all three just doesn't work or feel right.

You need good ambient light throughout that can provide a strong enough focus onto worktops without getting dirty. Good task lighting for preparing food on the worktops, and then good accent lighting on the dining table to provide an area of focused light to add a different layer and character to where you sit and eat. All three together is a match made in heaven.

Tasty

There are elements in making space that you can't really design, they kind of come after the bigger decisions are made, and these elements can be really tasty. I know what really makes a kitchen – it's all the little bits and bobs, such as cookbooks, for example. I love cookbooks – and we all have them – so find a place for them in your kitchen. They're a great way to bring a bit of soul into a room, so keep them nearby. If you use them a lot, think about a shelf somewhere that will take an open book to prevent it getting covered in sauce, flour, grease, etc.

Blackboard paint is a very cheap and easy way to keep shopping lists or school schedules in the forefront of your mind as it ensures these things are always on show. Or you can scribble up a recipe and read it while you cook. This can actually look very sharp if you really go for it.

Personalising a kitchen is what, for me, really makes for an amazing place to cook and eat. Good friends of mine have a large landscape painting over their sink – it sounds crazy, but it works. Hanging objects on blank walls can also add a graphical edge to the whole look, while also displaying some of your nice collectable items, which is always a good thing to do. Destroying a kitchen table can be fun. An old school table makes for a great family table that you won't be too precious about, so you won't care if paint spills on it because it will all add to its character, and a good linen table cloth will smarten it up for dinner if needs be.

"Personalising a kitchen is what, for me, really makes for an amazing place to cook and eat."

You might not be able to install a new kitchen, but this shouldn't stop you from changing the kitchen you have for the better. Painting kitchen doors and replacing a worktop can give a kitchen a much-needed facelift at very little cost.

If you have quite a traditional timber kitchen, you can spruce it up by painting it a sharp, contemporary colour (like deep-black–navy) and trim off some of the filigree cornices to give it a sharper look. This balances out the traditional style with a super modern colour and finish. Combine this with a new worktop and you're halfway to a new kitchen without the hassle or cost.

You can do a lot with what you already have, as my mother did in our own family home. We had a dark-brown timber-style kitchen with lead glass – it was stuck in the dark ages! But some new glass, new paint and a new worktop later and it was

Design: Dora Hurley; Image: Barbara Egan

unrecognisable. She supplemented it with a few larger larder units and a new hob as well. It looks great, like she has a new kitchen. I've enjoyed my Sunday roasts when visiting all the more since she took this on and she deserves great credit for the job she did.

The only real thing to remember is that cooking is about bringing people together, so it doesn't matter how small a space you have or if your budget is limited. Mark this down as your design brief and you will be guaranteed a better setup for making someone you love a cheese toasty when they really need one.

I suppose what I am really saying is, in the kitchen, don't forget who you are. Don't put the slick contemporary kitchen in if it is too sterile for you, or doesn't tie in to how you cook. Find out how you cook, who you are, what you like and then put it together. It doesn't have to be perfect; in fact, it's great if you can get it just imperfect enough.

DINING

Space will, of course, dictate what you can and can't do when it comes to dining. If space is tight, the breakfast table might have to double as the main dining table, and if this is the case, then I would plan for the latter. At the end of the day, all this has to be is a table, close to the kitchen with as many seats as you can comfortably fit around it.

Design: Kingston Lafferty Design; Image: Donal Murphy Photography

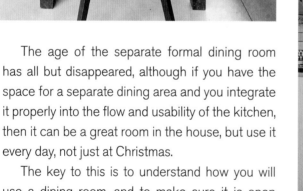

The age of the separate formal dining room has all but disappeared, although if you have the space for a separate dining area and you integrate it properly into the flow and usability of the kitchen, then it can be a great room in the house, but use it every day, not just at Christmas.

The key to this is to understand how you will use a dining room, and to make sure it is open and connected to the more lively kitchen space, otherwise it will become disjointed and will naturally segregate.

A separate dining room will also enable you to do something a little different that wouldn't necessarily

(Clockwise from top left) Design: ODKM Architects; Image: Infinity Media; Design/Image: Dulux (Bitter Chocolate 4 & Fire Cracker 5); Design: NOJI Architects; Image: Alice Clancy Photography

suit the everyday nature of a dining room that is part of the main kitchen space. You can add serious drama into a separate dining room if you are lucky enough to have the space. Low lighting, cool furniture, a touch of opulence – if you have it, you can really embrace Frank Lloyd Wright's take on dining as a real event.

I'm a great believer that if you design something right, it will be used. The rooms you see in a house that aren't 'used' are just not designed for what the owners need. I had a client who was building on a kitchen extension but who said they didn't want a 'formal' dining room because they'd had one and it was used twice a year to file the tax returns and on Christmas Day.

Their existing dining room opened into the living room and it was immediately clear that that dining room felt more part of the living room than the kitchen and so the dining space was just left in limbo. I knew they loved their food and with the right setup would certainly use a dining room properly because they entertained regularly. So we extended the kitchen and provided a new dedicated dining room to the rear and the existing underused dining room became a lounge area overlooking a new courtyard. They essentially ended up with the same series of rooms, but they were moved around and designed out and, as a result, they get used every day. Now they have a better living room along with the type of dining room they'd always wanted that fitted perfectly with their lifestyle. This just shows that sometimes the problem room isn't actually the problem.

If you are not extending, you can still incorporate the dining space into the kitchen, as long as you have the room to do so. Don't overcrowd the space with furniture that's too big – all you want here is an area that can comfortably seat four, six or eight people, depending on the size of the room. Sometimes a little corner that will seat two people comfortably is all a room needs.

Furniture

While I'm talking about furniture … as usual, there is plenty of choice but before you get to that, you have to think about what it needs to do.

If you have room to put a dining table within the kitchen space, then the key is to go big. Get the largest size that can comfortably fit – one that can seat eight at least – and keep it extended all the time. This not only gives the table the importance it needs because of its scale, but it also invites all kinds of activities to happen at it, sometimes at the same time at opposite ends. Painting, chatting, magazine reading, cup of tea drinking, shopping set down – this table is now your best friend. I think a good dining table shouldn't be too precious. If it is, it will feel like you can't use and abuse it every day. It should get a little scuffed and battered and should be part of the aesthetic.

From painting and colouring in with the kids, breakfast, lunch and dinner, drinking tea and catching up with whoever is cooking dinner right down to the Christmas poker game. This table sees so much action, and I always put it at the very centre of any home design – and you should too. Everything can happen at this table, to the degree that we often concentrate our design on this kitchen–dining relationship and forego the soft-seated lounge areas if space is tight, because this arrangement should take precedence over all else when it comes to creating alluring spaces to eat and drink and be together.

When it comes to dining chairs, you can mix and match, and have different styles and colours, but you shouldn't compromise on comfort. Ideally, a good chair should keep even the most delicate of bottoms comfortable all night long. Long, relaxed dinner parties with your mates or your family should happen here but, if you're not comfortable, then they won't. Of course, good posture is also required so always make sure the heights correspond with the table, and that there is a good balance of rigidity and comfort. I love an armrest on a dining chair because this brings it into the realm of an after-dinner conversation chair, and not just something to perch on until the meal is finished and you slink off somewhere else. I want to stay at the dinner table when the meal is done, when the conversation really begins.

Even though they don't have armrests, I also love bench seats as not only are they great for seating lots of people in a very simple way, they are also a very efficient use of what is normally 'dead' space in a room – the 450/500 mm right up against the wall.

A bench turns an unused narrow space up against a wall into a space-saving, crowd-pleasing social juggernaut. They can sit a row of kids at a party or a bunch of happy adults at dinner, and they often have storage space as well. They're a great way to maximise the efficiency of the space you have, and to get a good crowd of people around a dining table in a tight spot. Putting one in a corner is another clever way of making quite a generous dining table area in a smaller footprint. And, because you sit closer to one another on a bench, they are quite intimate and put people at ease.

Window seats

Graduating from a bench, you can have a bench within a large window, which will make a window seat. These can be particularly good if you love the outdoors, and you want to spend time in the garden, but, in Ireland, the weather maybe doesn't permit this as often as you would like. A good window seat will enable you to climb right into it, shoes off, feet up, and you should feel like you are sat outside. Again, they take up minimal space, but if you are able to incorporate one, you get something really unique. Anytime we have included a window seat in a project, the client always loves it. They seem to work particularly well in kitchens. People like to hang around kitchens – I think it's the promise of food that keeps us loitering – so the more spaces you can give to take a moment, annoy the chef and contemplate dinner, the better.

Design: Dean Cooper & Co; Image: Infinity Media

Nature

It makes sense to get the kitchen and dining spaces as close to an outdoor area as you can. Be it a garden, a balcony or a small internal courtyard, whatever it is, having your kitchen and dining space adjacent to this makes for easy indoor–outdoor dinners, and they are the obvious spaces to connect directly with the outdoors, maybe from a nice, large sliding door that really brings the outside in. Something I debate a lot with clients is that the kitchen and dining area is much more appropriate in the space directly adjacent to their garden, rather than the lounge seating area they were thinking of. Sometimes, people can get stuck in a way of living that they think is suitable for them, but it's just that they never had the opportunity to change it. For me, if you have a decent garden, it will always be better to position the kitchen and dining space next to it.

If you don't have a balcony or garden or courtyard, try to introduce some greenery on a windowsill or with some wall-mounted potted plants. They will completely change the feel of the room, and it will always add something different and unique. When I was renting in different flats around the UK as I was studying, I always made sure I had a green potted plant in the flat. A big one, at least a metre high. It added something soft, comforting and natural to the house that you really can't replicate and made it instantly feel like a home for me, even if I didn't have a sofa to sit on.

OPEN PLAN

Open-plan living really comes into force with the kitchen. If you are planning an extension or, indeed, just thinking about knocking through some walls to create the kitchen-dining-living space (KDL), you need to ensure it has the support spaces elsewhere in the house that will enable this space to work.

Connecting the kitchen and dining space in an open way is truly the best way to form a social and engaging space that makes the kitchen about more than just cooking. Don't listen to anyone who is worried about cooking smells because this can be dealt with by a good extractor fan. Whatever kind of kitchen you are going for, this connectivity should be at the core of what you are doing.

A family with three kids will not survive in one large, open-plan kitchen-dining-living space if there is no other room to support this space when some separate time is needed. My sister has an open-plan, L-shaped KDL space and it works really well; we spend most of our time there, eating lunch and playing with the kids – all four of them – so it's pretty mad most of the time. There is another room though, a separate television room, and this is critical support for the KDL. It enables respite from the madness, for the kids as much as the adults, and this is why the other space is so successful. I have been to houses that have opened up the back of the house completely, and despite it being vast in size, it doesn't work because everyone has to be there all of the time, and as we all know that isn't always a good thing!

Zoning

The open-plan KDL is a great space if you can do it – it is the single most requested item on most clients' wish lists. There is a subtlety to carrying it off successfully though, and it is imperative that each area feels like its own 'zone' within the space. What I mean is, you shouldn't feel like you're sitting on a sofa in the kitchen, or that you are cooking in the middle of the living room. Each space is different, and has different criteria, so they should be clearly defined and respond to this.

There are lots of tricks to help you achieve this. Changing ceiling heights is a great way to define different zones within one larger space, along with a change in floor level. A few steps up or down into a lounge area can completely change the way a space feels, and make it feel slightly removed from the larger space while still being part of it. A degree of disconnect is desirable, and it is this balance you are looking for. You want to avoid rattling around a big square box at the back of the house, so it needs to be clearly thought-out so that it's not too open.

When designing out an open-plan space, it is important to look at each individual space and design it through fully, so you get a feel for the appropriate size and shape of each zone within the bigger space. There's nothing worse than being in a big open-plan extension to the back of a house that is just not working. Everything is conflicting and there is no clarity in design. This is *not* open-plan design. This is just bad design.

Open plan is considered and clever. Furniture has room to breathe, the flow is effortless, and people can feel open or closed within the one space. It shouldn't bare

Design: De Siún Scullion Architects; Image: Philip Lauterbach Photography

all or be one-dimensional, it should still maintain elements of privacy and quietness. This is what gives it the layers it needs to function.

The key to designing a good open-plan space is to really get to grips with what's happening in each area, so really try to visualise this. Draw your furniture in the space to give it scale, as you want connection between spaces, but a little hidden corner or a window seat out of view is a lovely way to gain a touch of privacy which these spaces need. L-shaped plans are great for this as they are open and connected but easily definable as separate areas, and it is this balance that works best.

Furniture plays a key role in an open-plan space, as it can define a room and direct its flow – these are subtle things but absolutely critical in making a space feel correct. Don't get too much in there either, let the space feel open.

Half walls, up to 1.1 metres in height, can act as sculptural barriers to hide views or areas of seating. You can still see over the top of them, but can also put a sofa on the other side to hunker down and watch television. Bookcases are another great way to break up and define spaces, and you can leave them open so you can sneak a peak through different parts of the room without seeing everyone all at once. Free-standing walls can also add a little visual interest and help define different spaces. These need not go all the way across a room, sometimes just a 1.5 metre-long wall can direct and break up space just enough to make it work.

wash

Bathing. It is one of life's great pleasures and, I have to say, we have really lost our way when it comes to celebrating the bathroom and the joy and peace it can bring. Bathing used to be an event – centuries ago, we used to gather in bathhouses as part of our culture and society, it was a social event and we met to talk amongst our peers and friends. While communal bathing is not as openly practised as it used to be, after a long and hard day, most of us still love to sink into a bath or take a long shower, literally washing the day away. I start and end every day with a long shower, and it's a precious time of the day for me. There is something spiritual in it. Water is a vital element for our survival, and we have a strong connection to it.

The removing of clothes, the feeling of water over your body, is an intimate form of cleansing that runs deep, and the thought of doing this in a cramped, badly lit en-suite literally makes me fume. People have put the onus on how many bathrooms they can fit into their home, or how many en-suites, for the purpose of potential resale value, and all the while they are compromising their daily life in the house. I will always choose a good-sized main bathroom over a smaller version with a tiny cramped and dark en-suite. I don't see the value this adds to a home, either in the joy

Design: Maxime Laroussi/Urban Agency; Images: Barbara Egan

of living there every day or indeed in the resale of it in the future.

Space and light is what adds value to a home, and a badly designed and badly laid out en-suite has neither.

We all want more bathrooms in our homes, but I think we have been brainwashed. Along the way, nobody thought to stop and actually question the real value these kinds of spaces actually add. Certainly, a good en-suite in the right location is brilliant when you can do it, but if you can't, don't force it. First and foremost, a house should have a decent-sized family bathroom, and the introduction of an en-suite should be looked at if possible.

I walked away from a large period restoration project because the client was insisting on locating an en-suite within the main bedroom, which would have totally compromised the formal proportions of the room. Our relationship with bathrooms is confused; we're obsessed with them, but for all the wrong reasons.

For this reason, I'm actually quite pleased with the resurgence in creating some form of home spa in the bathroom, which is becoming more popular. I think we are beginning to realise that enjoying your home is what everyone should concentrate on. While I think a home spa can be a little over the top, the sentiment it is striving for is all good for me. It's trying to get us to rediscover that spending time in the bathroom is a good thing, for our minds as well as our bodies, and we should have a bathroom that makes us happy, and that we can spend a good deal of time in.

It's a difficult challenge as the demands on the design process are high. Bathrooms are usually smaller spaces, so how do we get what we need in there without it becoming cramped? What exactly should we put in there?

There's a lot of services to get in there too, from plumbing to mechanical ventilation. If you're a big music lover it can be a great place to build in some speakers, or even a shower radio if you want to liven things up a little. Whatever it is, never let go of the demand for your bathroom to give you some sort of pleasure. Bathing is no longer the mundane utility it once was. We need to free ourselves from this and embrace its potential for enjoyment. The design challenge should be to make a space that you can comfortably spend forty-five minutes in, so here's what to consider.

LAYOUT

Hopefully by now you are beginning to understand that everything begins with layout, because when you get this right, everything else can follow. Think about what functions will be required in the room.

If you are redoing your bathroom, go back to square one and redesign it from scratch. It will add real value to your home and, if it was laid out a few generations ago, it could probably do with a fresh approach. The major change will be in relocating the toilet if you have to. If it's fine where it is, then including a good walk-in shower or even introducing a concealed cistern with modern finishes and good lighting will give your bathroom a serious makeover.

If you have just the one room and it's small, then you will have to compromise, but don't compromise on light, ergonomics and comfort. A beautifully designed, small wet room can do everything a bathroom should and still be a pleasurable and relaxing place. You should ask yourself lots of questions to establish what you need, or want, to include in your bathroom. Think about what you do in the bathroom.

- How much storage do I need in the bathroom?
- Do I want a shower and a bath?
- Will I build in the bath or have it free-standing?
- Do I have room to separate both?
- What kind of shower tray do I need?
- Should this be a wet room?
- Is there enough room for a chair? (This can be really handy.)
- Is there a need for a toilet here or is there one somewhere else?
- What style of toilet would work best? Pedestal, wall hung or flush back?
- What style of sink would work best? Free-standing? Built-in?
- How do I want to store toiletries? Around the sink? A shelf? A cabinet?
- How do I want to store toiletries in the shower or by the bath?
- Where will the towels go? Do I need a shelf for them?
- Should I have a towel rail or a radiator?
- Should I have underfloor heating?

Storage in the bathroom need not be overly large, it just needs to be in the right position.

The questions can be endless but answering the ones above is a good place to start.

I would encourage you to really examine the proportions of the room and respond to them. You can't fit a round peg through a square hole, so if your bathroom is a small space, don't try to get a free-standing bath in there. The bathroom layout should be appropriate for its size, so that it feels comfortable in the space.

New bathrooms on existing first-floor levels should be tested to ensure the existing joists can take the additional loads. A cast-iron free-standing bath, full to the brim, with two adults in it will test most floor build-ups, so if you are renovating a bathroom in an existing house, and it has timber joists (as most do), then make sure you check the load and allow for additional splicing in the joists to accommodate the increased loading if necessary.

You may not necessarily have to accommodate all these functions into one space, in fact it can be rather nice if you don't. If you have a separate toilet, this can often free up the main bathroom, which is useful in the mornings if you have a busy family. A small toilet downstairs, even under the stairs, is always useful for visiting guests so they don't have to intrude upstairs into more private areas of your house.

If you're feeling particularly brave, you can have your en-suite as a shower or bath within the main bedroom, with no walls or divisions – you see this in hotels sometimes but I'm not sure it's for everyone! Usually, this would be a free-standing bath or a large shower and a wash hand basin, and the WC is located elsewhere. This might not suit everyone but you can play around with a less conventional layout if you have to, and you can make it work. Anything is possible.

BATH

I rarely take baths as they drain me because of the heat. I don't find them energising, but that's just me. When I am training for a marathon or an adventure race, I take quite a few baths, but they are filled with iced water and they aren't overly pleasant either. In saying all of this, I do think every home should have a bath, and a decent one at that. They add something to a home, something comforting, something homely.

The average size for a bath is approximately 1,700 mm x 700 mm, but the bigger you can get, the better. If possible, go for central tap mounts on the bath so two people can lie in it comfortably without drawing straws to see who sits up against the taps. A free-standing bath will take up much more space, so bear that in mind and measure to ensure your bathroom can accommodate one. If you can fit one, free-standing baths

(Top) Design: Tilestyle; Image: Dúira Photography; (Bottom) © ariadna de raadt/Shutterstock.com

look great at an angle as you enter the room, and preferably near a window too.

If you are going for a standard bath, a good tip is to spend a little on tiling it in place instead of fixing the plastic panel on the side. This does a number of things. It removes the wobbly bit of plastic, but it also grounds the bath and makes it look and feel much more secure and solid, and therefore luxurious. You can do this with timber as well if you want, but I am always impressed when we tile a bath into place as it has an immediate effect on the space, transforming it from plastic to fantastic. It's one of my key tips in the bathroom, to the point that there is no turning back – this is the way we fit baths now.

There are plenty of toys for the bathroom, just like the kitchen. Saunas, water jets, jacuzzis and whirlpools. My only piece of advice with

this is to get something as subtle as possible – we've all walked into a bathroom that was plush in its day, but the whirlpool looks like it is stuck in a time warp. If you have to have a massaging bath, keep it subtle.

SHOWER

As you may have guessed by the fact that I take two a day, I love a good shower, in fact it is part of my holy trinity of good living. In terms of luxuries in the bathroom, I tend to forget the toys and concentrate on putting in a big generous shower, for two if space permits. There is nothing more luxurious than space. I hold this true in every design I do, but it's particularly challenging in bathrooms, and specifically showers because, more often than not, space is tight. My rule is to put in as big a shower as you can, you won't regret it.

Often, just a slight jump from the standard shower size can make a big difference to how a bathroom feels, and the additional cost can be very little in comparison to the benefits (remember, value versus cost).

If the shower is the only option for bathing in the house then it is even more reason to ensure it is as good and generous as you can make it. I would make a lot

Design: Martins Camisuli Architects; Image: Jake Fitzjones Photography

of design sacrifices to ensure I had a generous shower, no matter what – it's that important.

Splurge on a quality shower head to give you a proper rinsing in the morning. Depending on water pressure a pump may need to be installed, or you may want to think about changing your boiler to help with pressure.

Whatever you are thinking about, make sure to clearly describe it to the plumber and make sure you use a reputable supplier who can advise you on the technicalities involved in the installation of the sanitary ware.

Plumbing can be expensive, so it's worth getting to grips with the terminology to ensure you know that everything has been covered. I remember a recent project where the supplier sold a system to our client knowing full well that a diverter switch (the switch that diverts water from the main shower head to a hand-held shower) was not included. When the plumber saw the system, he presumed a single shower was all that was required, based on what had been supplied. The system was installed, and everyone found themselves in a tricky position where the client didn't get what they thought they were buying and it wasn't the contractor's fault. This happened in all three bathrooms in the house and they were all tiled before we noticed the omission. We had to break open all the tiles and buy the proper systems to retro-fit them. Time and money wasted, literally down the drain. I now draw the shower setup on the wall with the plumber to make sure we are all singing off the same hymn sheet.

Shower trays have become so slim that the old stigma they once had as being clunky and difficult to step over has all but disappeared. They can be almost flush with the floor finish, and the change in material under foot can be quite pleasant. People can feel that a wet room is the best solution because they still feel a shower tray doesn't look great, but look closely at the newest ranges of shower trays, before you make a decision because you will be pleasantly surprised.

There are other options, of course. You can tile the bottom of your shower with a small step into it, or use a step to demarcate a different section in the room. This sounds a bit odd but it works, if you are happy with the step. What it is doing is actually extending the raised shower tray level outwards to give an entrance platform from which to enter the shower. It's very clever really. In design terms, I call this running with the problem and designing it out. If I can't change the floor level in a bathroom to get a wet room or walk-in shower, then I will try something like this. Either way, don't let the problem beat you.

Alternatively, a wet room is the right solution in certain circumstances. They need to be thought through because the falls in the floor need to be worked out in advance – this will also affect your tiling layouts and design for runoff. Their main advantage is that, as there is no shower tray, the floor finish can continue into the shower, giving a sense of openness that makes the room feel bigger. They can also look very slick because you can maintain one or two materials throughout the floor and wall finish. Usually, a fixed glass screen is required to contain some of the splashback and, depending on size, a retractable or sliding door may be needed. They can also be very easy to clean, and if you have one downstairs they can be used for hosing down pets, kids and wellies.

SINKS

A little bit of extra size here goes a long way. The ideal hand basin area should be big enough to have a good spread of lotions, toothpaste and products splayed out now and again, with a good mirror above it and eye-level lighting to either side or from above. This should form part of a vanity unit that can store all the lotions when not in use. From brushing teeth, shaving, applying makeup and washing our hands, quite a lot happens at a basin, so it should be able to cope.

Storage can come from above with a wall-mounted unit, preferably with a mirror finish, or it can go underneath. Again, room size will dictate what will work best. In a small en-suite, a wall-hung vanity unit will keep the floor free and make the space look bigger. This can contain a small amount of storage, and with a wall-mounted mirror above and good lighting, that's all you really need.

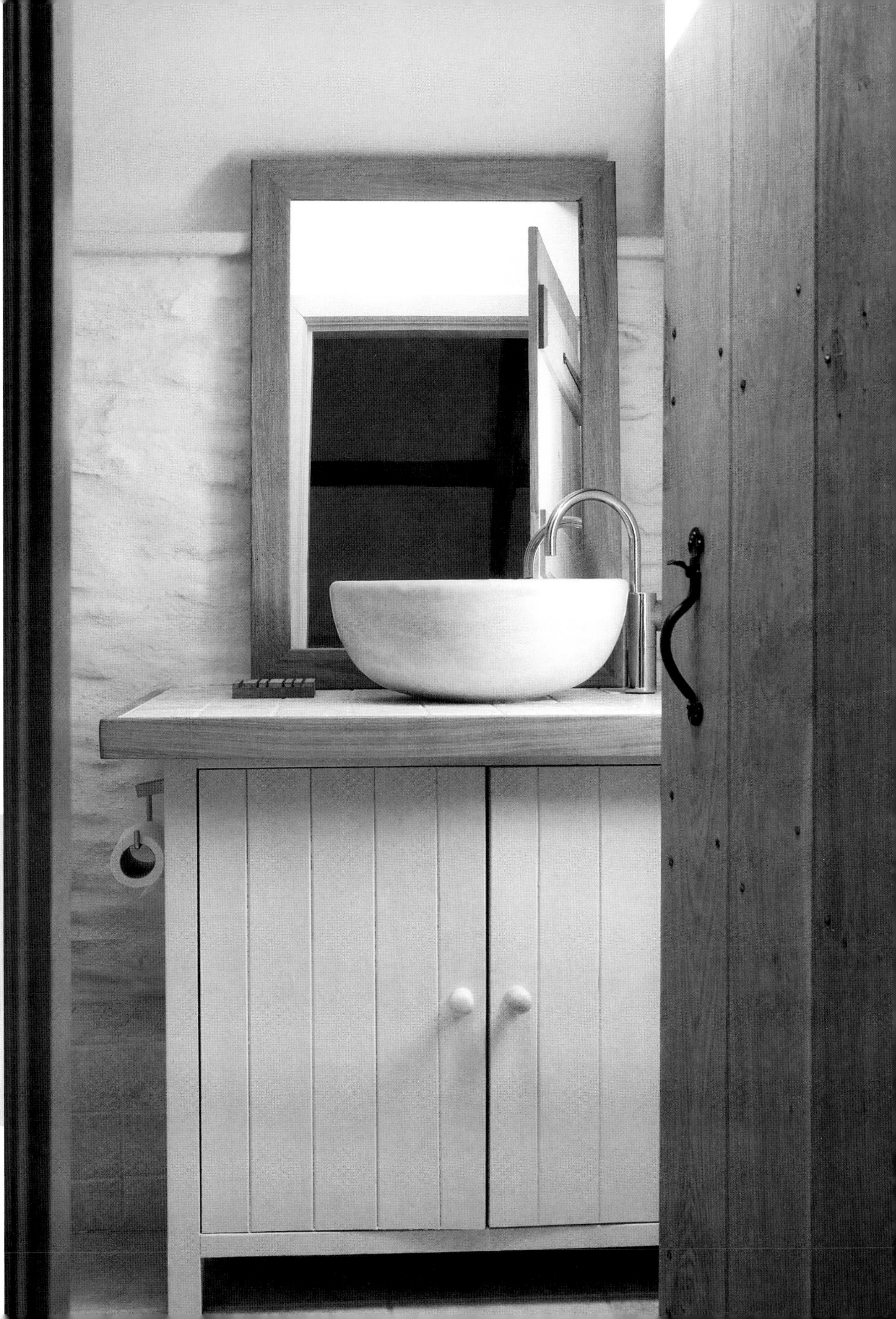

TOILETS

The toilet will form a partnership with the other sanitary ware in your bathroom, and a lot of the same decisions need to be made. The golden rule still applies though: keep it simple. The first decision is about the plumbing for the toilet: should the cistern be exposed or concealed? Concealing it can look great, and you can incorporate this into the vanity unit build-up. Essentially this means building out a stud wall to house the cistern, but when space is really tight don't run this to the ceiling; instead, just form a simple shelf and put a nice big mirror backing on it. This gives you the concealed look, and a very usable shelf and a large mirror. I've done this a few times and it always works very well.

Wall-mounted toilets generally work best to free up the floor space for ease of cleaning and to make the space appear bigger, which is usually on the design brief. This is a decision that needs to be made early on, as structural work is required to the wall to house the unit, so this all has to happen before you tile the wall.

There are no real rules in bathrooms, as there are in kitchens, just the basics of functionality, flow and ergonomics.

FITTINGS

As in the kitchen, I would advise spending money on the taps and door handles – the things we touch. This means a very simple white bathroom can be elevated with a snazzy tap or an oversized showerhead. You can mount taps on the wall, something we often forget about in bathrooms, and this can tie in well with a concealed cistern or shelf that houses the workings of the systems, so all that is seen are the clean lines of the units themselves.

LIGHTING

As you know, I am obsessed with lighting, and lighting in bathrooms is probably the worst thing I see when I visit people's homes. We seem to have decided that one large pendant light in a bathroom is all we need. Madness. More often than not, the lighting setup is similar to that of a cupboard.

Lighting in a bathroom is simple. Good ambient lighting on a dimmer will be enough to wash the space in a gentle layer of light, with specific task lighting concentrated on the mirror – either from above or, ideally, from each side. We light almost every bathroom mirror from the side as it's the optimum way to light the human face, ideal for shaving, brushing teeth, applying makeup or just admiring yourself. This is why actors have those mirrors with round bulbs around the edge. These lights should be operated on a separate light switch so you can turn just them on if you wish. LED strips are great to put along concealed surfaces, on the top or underneath storage units to give a bit of drama and luxury to the space – and it's so simple and cheap to do. A bit of thought into lighting will transform your bathroom.

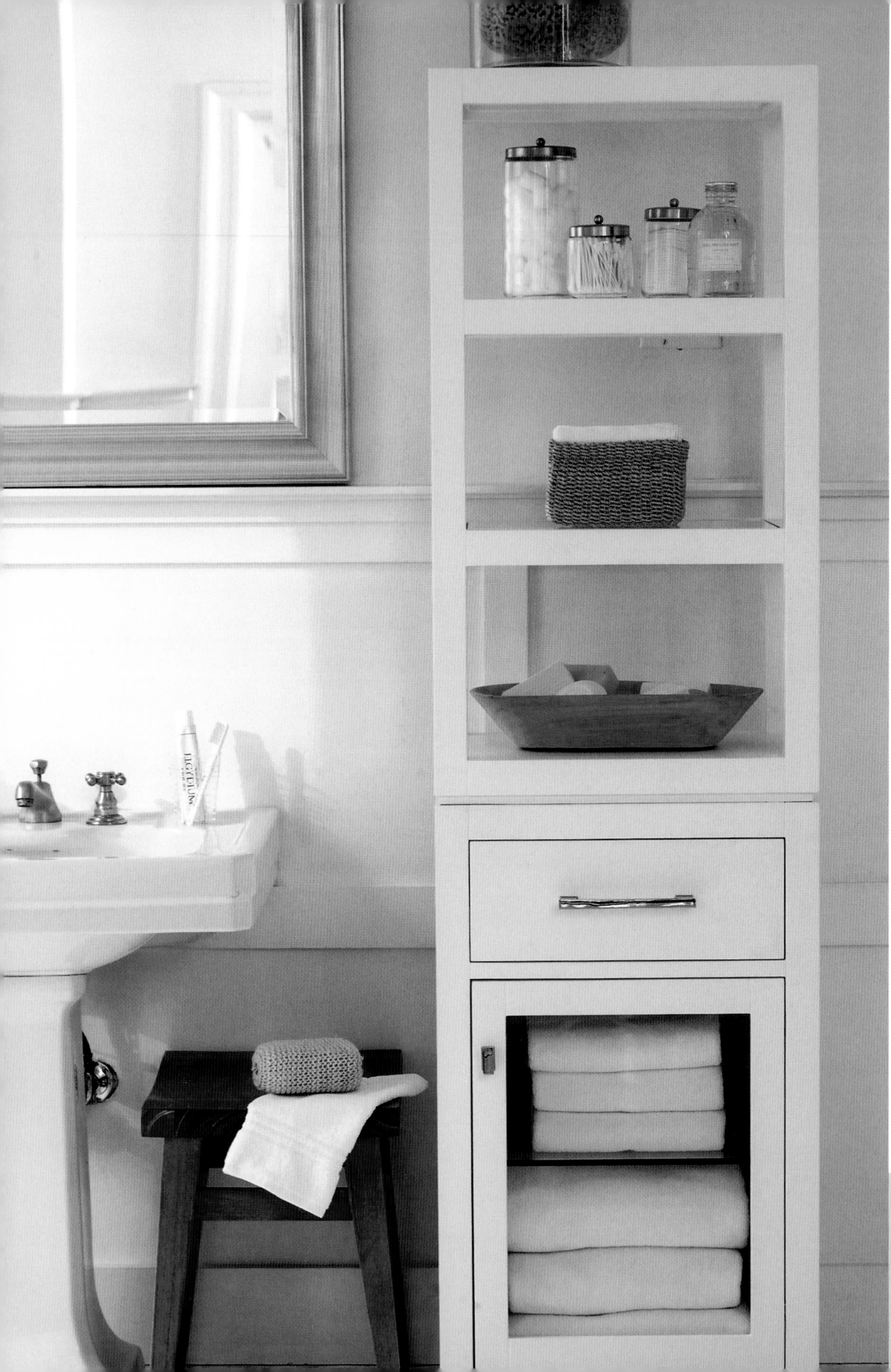

© Getty Images/Rick Lew

STORAGE

I would always advise having storage within the vanity unit and along a shelf of some sort, recessed and within easy reach of the sink. If your bathroom is big enough to take some additional storage when you have these established, then great. This can be open to display and clearly show where towels and toiletries are, or it can be closed off to free up some towel, toiletry and cleaning storage from other areas of the house. A well-positioned chair can do some of this for you, and sometimes it's nice to take a moment to sit and relax when you get out of the shower.

FLOORS AND WALLS

Mosaic tiles can look great on the floors and the walls and, in particular, in wet rooms, where they take up the difference in the sloping floor that larger tiles cannot. Always check the slip resistance of tiles as not all tiles can be used on the floor as well as the wall. I think natural materials tend to work best in bathrooms. Stone and porcelain tiles are the usual choices and they have a quality that will not diminish over time.

Timber can be great to use in the vanity unit or along a storage wall to bring warmth to areas that are away from the concentrated areas of water. Light, dark, bright or muted – fill your bathroom with joy and express yourself.

WINDOWS

A quick word about windows. Try to ensure you have a window, or at least a skylight, in your bathroom. Natural light in a bathing space is pure joy. In fact, I absolutely love having an open window in a shower if I can get one. When I lived in London, even during the coldest days, I opened my shower window every day to get that mix of hot water and cold air that is the freshest of wake-up calls. Pure bliss.

Depending on the bathroom's proximity to adjoining neighbours, you may have to use opaque glass in a bathroom or en-suite so don't forget to check what and who you can see from your bathroom window and, more importantly, who may be able to see in.

sleep

Some bedrooms are all about the view. If you are lucky enough to have a panoramic outlook with big windows, then being able to lie in bed and look out at nature is one of life's great pleasures.

The bedroom is perhaps the most important room in your house. You might be surprised to hear that, given that we think of kitchens and living rooms as the main rooms, but the bedroom is where you start and finish every day. Every. Day. They are a place of rest when you need it, comforting you when you're ill, and a room removed from the busy life that is shared with many.

A good night's sleep is essential for our health, but lots of things can get in the way of that – sound, light, temperature, comfort. In fact, any of these are often the result of bad design and, in the spirit of fighting fire with fire, all you need is some good design to turn things around. In this room, of all rooms, you owe it to your health to embrace good design to make it the best it can be.

Often, bedrooms are the most overlooked when it comes to home renovations but, with a little thought, it's the one place you can add a little bit of luxury and decadence to create a space that's completely your own.

Design: Studio Red Architects; Image: Peter Grogan/Emagine

ORIENTATION

If possible, the bedrooms should be located at quieter ends of the house, away from the main doors and living areas, for obvious reasons. An east-facing orientation is great, as you will rise with the morning sun.

Generally our bedrooms are upstairs for security and privacy, but upside-down houses flip this notion, usually to take advantage of a view or an elevated site. This can work as long as you can maintain that element of safety and privacy on the ground floor so you really need a clever layout that still enables you to enter on ground level and draw you upstairs to the living areas.

Bedrooms should also be close to a bathroom for midnight trips to the loo, so this poses big questions in examining your current arrangement of rooms to see if they are working properly for you.

When it comes to the bedroom itself, if you can, position your bed adjacent to a window. Some people find that a bed directly facing an opposing window is a bit too much as they can't help but feel someone might be looking in. It's a subconscious, psychological thing, but it's something that's directly connected to the act of falling asleep. A good blind system may alleviate any concerns. Similarly, placing a bed directly under a window is not advised either. With existing layouts and access into bedrooms this is sometimes unavoidable, but if you have a choice, go for the adjacent bed position.

"An east-facing orientation is great, as you will rise with the morning sun."

When you have that sorted, all you need is a simple bedside locker at each side, enough to hold a couple of books and maybe a light (more on that later). You need plenty of sockets at each side of the bed for any alarm clocks, lights, etc., though I recommend you plug your phone in elsewhere in the room to stop you screen-gazing at bedtime, on a set of drawers or a windowsill maybe (that's where I put mine). That's it. Everything else in the bedroom can be worked out after you get this simple setup right.

As a general tip, an element of symmetry in where the bed goes is useful as it adds a restful and grounded feeling to the room.

All the elements of a good bedroom are on display here. Big warm rug for your feet, lighting and tables at each side of the bed, a chair for clothes or putting on your shoes, a headboard to give focus to the bed and all set off with nice big cushions. Simple stuff, but it makes all the difference.

Design/Image: © Ebony and Co

WINDOWS

As bedrooms are night-time and daytime rooms, how you dress the windows is particularly important. Personally, I love the brightness of summer beaming through my window, even at 5.30 a.m. Although I am absolutely not a morning person, it's a lovely way to wake up, and an eye mask usually sorts me out for the following hour before I get up. We are naturally in tune with the passing of day and night, as it is linked to our biological clock, so waking up to the sun is the most natural thing in the world.

Some people prefer blackout blinds all year round. These are simple to put together, all you need is a combination of double-lined curtains with a blackout shade fixed to the back. If you have to have curtains in the bedroom, run them to the ground, and fix them as high to the ceiling as you can. This will elongate them, so you get a solid section of fabric from top to bottom – a much more elegant solution that going to the top of the window.

Shutters are another great way of keeping the day away, and add character without the need for any soft furnishings. A mix of dressings is sometimes desirable because of the changing seasons. Soft linen blinds allow a lovely diffuse light into a room, while still giving privacy. These can be great in the summer, but you might want something a little more sturdy for the winter months, so combining these with larger curtains to the side or with shutters could provide the ideal combination.

BED

The starting point with any bedroom is the chariot itself, the bed. Layout will dictate what type of bed you can get, so measure the room and see what size bed will fit. Another golden rule is to get the biggest bed you can comfortably fit into the space, and it's the width that's important, not the length. Unless you're six-foot plus, a standard-length bed will suffice, around 1,500 mm x 2,000 mm but the real luxury comes when you opt for something a bit wider. While we all love sharing a bed, sometimes we all just need a little extra room to roll around in.

When you have established what size it can be, think about what type of bed you want. Would a low-level bed suit the space or do you prefer something a bit higher? Either way, the ideal bed will have equal measures of comfort and support. Mattress quality is really what we're talking about here, and this is one area not to scrimp on. Buy the best you can afford and it is worth making a couple of other sacrifices to get the most supportive and comfortable one you can find. We spend a third of our lives in bed so make sure yours is a good one.

Layering different textures in the bedroom is vital for increased comfort. It is also an opportunity to bring some life and colour into the room with cushions and blankets – so you can really up the style stakes in the bedroom.

What do you do in bed?

It's a personal question, but one you need to ask of yourself. As with all rooms in the house, we love to build flexibility into the bedroom. This allows us to carry out a number of tasks in the room, in the process (hopefully) helping to avoid arguments. The only real answers that I feel are appropriate to the above question are: sleep, read … and the other thing – and, no, I don't mean watching TV!

Digital technology has revolutionised how we live. It infiltrates our every activity and, in some cases, the activity is no longer possible without it. This is generally a good thing and it has changed all our lives, but – and it is a big but – as any doctor will tell you, we all need to start unplugging ourselves from all this technology before we go to bed. Plug in the phones out of reach, on a ledge or windowsill, and keep the television downstairs where it belongs. It's a simple tip but you'll love the benefits.

Seating

Depending on the size of your room, if you can, a small place to sit is a wonderful thing. When we walk into a hotel room and gush at how lovely it is, it's usually only a little bigger than a standard double bedroom – it's just laid out better. A small seated area, or even a well-positioned, big, comfortable chair and side table can make all the difference. It enables you to spend time in the bedroom that's not in bed. It makes things like putting on your shoes easier and, when you feel like it, you can throw your clothes all over it – just don't let it turn into a clothes horse. It's a great place for an early-morning cup of tea or a late-night chat waiting for someone to get out of the shower. Great if you can have it.

The master bedroom is one of the primary rooms in a house and the more space you can get into it, the better it will function.

(Left) © Worldwide/Shutterstock.com; (Right) © photobank.ch/Shutterstock.com

DRESSING

While a separate dressing room is a luxury that few can have, how we store, access and close off clothing storage is a big part of the success of any bedroom. Using the hotel setup again, they really have this one nailed. If space is tight, you might opt for running one long built-in unit 600 mm in depth along one wall, getting everything you need into it. This will always be the most space-efficient solution, and this can also have folding doors to create a small seated vanity unit with a mirror, giving you the best of both worlds.

Design: Dean Cooper & Co; Image: Infinity Media

Bigger rooms enable the use of free-standing pieces at different locations. If we had to, I am sure we could fit the clothes we need into a standard 1,800 mm-wide floor-to-ceiling unit. If you have enough clothes to fill a whole room, then you should think about incorporating a dressing room into your bedroom design.

If you have the space, knocking through to an adjacent, lesser used room can make absolutely huge differences to your bedroom layout. The reason for this is that it enables storage (clothes) to be located elsewhere, so you can concentrate solely on the bed and the act of sleeping in the main bedroom.

LIGHTING

People often don't realise the importance of lighting in a bedroom to create a successful room; a lack of natural light or simply bad artificial lighting can both cause problems.

What do you do with a dark bedroom? If you can, introduce new windows, as this is the best way to pull in more light. Be careful with planning issues to the front and side, but if your bedroom is to the back of the house it's worth the effort because this is the most dramatic way of changing the light in a room. What about the ceiling? Can you go up into the attic and expose the rafters and get a big roof light in? This

> "If you can, introduce new windows, as this is the best way to pull in more light."

can add drama and light into the room and, if you have the space, you could get a ladder up to the space and utilise it as a dressing room or a chill-out area within the bedroom. Now we're talking!

If you can't get natural light into your room, don't just write it off as a dark room that is beyond help. It's all about artificial lighting to create a mood and atmosphere. You can still have the most amazing bedroom even if it gets limited natural light.

Harsh central lights have no place in a bedroom, and the correct setup is relatively simple to do, so there should be no excuse not to do it. As with other rooms, good ambient lighting on dimmer switches is enough to give you ample light for getting around. This can be either the main central light, or an LED strip under some built-in units.

It is in how the task lighting is incorporated that the real magic happens. Bedside lights, either long hung pendants, wall lights or just simple table lamps that can be switched on a separate loop (from the entrance wall and beside the bed) will give a lovely warm glow to the space that is just very alluring in the bedroom.

Having these lights on separate switches means you don't have to fall out over who gets up on a cold night to turn the light off. It also makes reading in bed much easier and, if one of you can't sleep, then one light can stay on a little longer than the other without disturbing your slumbering partner. It's such a simple thing to do, and it just makes life easier.

Clever storage

If there's one thing that can lower the feel-good factor of any bedroom, it's clutter and mess, so a good storage system is essential, it's the first step in creating the oasis of calm you want in your room. There are lots of ways to improve storage in bedrooms. Although having a bedside table at each side of the bed works very well, you could also run a compact unit along the back of the bed. You can open shelving directly onto the bed, which will give lots of extra space for linens, books and alarm clocks. It also gives you a nice big shelf behind the bed for lights or speakers. It's a

Design: Dean Cooper & Co; Image: Infinity Media

Design: Dean Cooper & Co; Image: Infinity Media

Luxury if you can have it –
a separate dressing room
not only keeps all your
clothes organised, it also
frees up the bedroom itself.

great way of getting in extra space where you think there isn't any. For clothes, do you have a small but well-thought-out wardrobe so some open storage would be appropriate or do you just want everything tucked away behind a closed door for convenience?

Built-in and free-standing

Depending on the size of your project, or what room proportions you are working with, a key question is often whether to build in some storage or go with free-standing units. There's no right or wrong answer here, but there is always context (budget, room size, etc.) so some rules will apply.

Generally speaking, building units into a space will be the most efficient way of maximising the storage available in an area. It also means you can design something that will work within the confines of a given shape, and you can tailor its shelf sizes to your specific needs. If you go with full-height doors, you can get a very sleek and minimal look with bags of concealed storage behind. This isn't always possible, but it's great if you can do it.

Free-standing pieces often work in either bigger spaces (that can take large single pieces) or, funnily enough, in really small spaces. Wardrobes are something we all

> "Building units into a space will be the most efficient way of maximising the storage available in an area."

struggle with, and the best one I have seen in small spaces was an open rack displaying a limited selection of clothes. You can supplement this with a chest of drawers elsewhere, but this is a solution for when space is tight. This brings colour to the room, but it feels spacious and open – key characteristics if you have a small bedroom. In every project I do, there is usually a mix of both built-in and free-standing storage – so it will depend on the room, size and quantity of storage required.

Every day BUT not everyday

If you find the storage wars all too much to handle, this is a simple trick to keep in mind. Think about how you store the items you will need every day (like socks) versus things you will not need every day (like a spare duvet), and then design your storage around this.

Depending on your lifestyle, your storage needs will be different from other people's, so it's actually a really important thing to get right. It should be every bit as bespoke as the rest of your home.

Just the tiniest difference can sometimes be the missing ingredient to a perfectly comfortable and usable space. Even coat hooks in bedrooms can bring a bit of life and keep things close to hand as you leave in the morning. Small ideas – big difference.

KIDS

In complete contrast to the above, the rules for kids and their bedrooms change as they get older and need different things, so be prepared for this to happen.

Babies and young children need certain pieces of furniture and furnishings to enable you to complete the day-to-day tasks involved in looking after them – a

changing table, cot and somewhere to store their clothes. If you have the space to include a chair, this can be very useful for you, for things like feeding and reading to your child. Beyond this, try and bring lots of colour into the room and lots of different textures. This can be done with rugs, and cushions. But remember that babies and very young children don't spend much time in their rooms, so there is no need to do too much.

As your children get older, they will become more vocal about how they want their rooms to be. It will start to be a place where they play, hang out with friends, do their homework, and so the furniture in it will need to adapt to these changing needs. Younger children may need more storage for toys, and a big box into which everything can be put helps with a quick tidy-up at the end of the day. As always, start with the layout of the room and think about what happens in the room; children do a lot more in their rooms than just sleep.

If the room is not very big, a mid-high or high bed that incorporates a desk, chair and storage underneath can solve a lot of problems for older children.

Letting your children decorate their bedrooms is a great way of helping them express their personalities, and it's great to let them reflect their interests – even if they won't let you in the room. When I was a teenager, my own bedroom was filled with posters, all kinds of crazy lights, a life-sized, cardboard cut-out of Han Solo and a couple of guitars. Your child may ask you to paint their room black (I did) so, if they do, let them and see what happens!

extending your home

Building an extension can be a great way to fix problems with your home and make it tailored specifically for you. It gives you an opportunity to do something really special, to create a place that truly inspires – a special place, made just for you. This is why I love to work on extending someone's home.

Extensions are a fertile ground for architects, and I think in Ireland we have some of the best and brightest at turning existing homes into truly world-class pieces of domestic architecture. It never ceases to amaze me what is possible to do with a standard three-bed semi. A good extension will add everything to your home, practically and financially, and give you a design for life to enjoy. A bad extension will do the complete opposite, and can turn your much-hoped-for dream home into a bit of a nightmare, so there are pitfalls to avoid and things to consider before you take it on.

You might be surprised to hear that building an extension is one of the toughest jobs an architect will face – new builds are easy by comparison. The reason is that you are adding on a new structure and trying to stitch it back into an existing (and much older) building, yet they must sit happily together as one and operate as one functioning machine.

Most people want to do something with their homes, and extending is often at the top of that list. The need for more space is the obvious driver, but this might be possible to gain back without extending. A good architect will look at every room in the house (even if you've never mentioned them!), as sometimes a reorganisation of internal spaces can do much more than you think.

We always do this as part of our initial design stage, to establish what works and what doesn't in the house. We look at the entire floorplan in conjunction with a client's design brief and see what's possible in the existing house first. An extension is only worth doing if you have all other rooms figured out and resolved. An extension that makes other rooms obsolete in the house is not the right answer – they must all be part of the same thing. They can't compete with one another as this will only end in more dead space.

Find the problems, unlock the potential, get your house in order and then get to work on the extension. If there are problem rooms in the house then this is the time to fix them.

If you are already at maximum efficiency with every room being used, and you're still having issues, then that is the right time to think about adding on more space and, of course, more value to your home.

(Top) Design: NOJI Architects; Image: Alice Clancy Photography; (Bottom) Design/Image: Carson & Crushell Architects

Building an extension is a great opportunity to fix everything in your home, and create something truly unique, that is specifically tailored just for your needs.

ORIENTATION

I've mentioned orientation a few times already, but it's something that needs to be considered. The key with any extension is to be very aware of the orientation and the path of sunlight because you will want to capture as much of this as possible, especially if you are significantly remodelling the internal layout of your house as well. Adding on large structures will obviously impact on the natural light in the house, so the design of the new extension

should respond to this; make sure it doesn't cast shadows into existing rooms or gardens. If you have a favourite spot that gets lovely sun in the evening, be careful you manage this and don't ruin it.

DO IT ONCE, DO IT RIGHT

I always say that you can spend a good €50,000 or a bad €50,000 on the same house at any given time, and it's true. Your home is the largest investment you are likely to make and you need to take time and consider carefully what the best options for you are in terms of how to upgrade or improve it.

Something that always generates lots of debate is how an extension or a new building will look in its given context and landscape. For this, it's the materials that matter – below is a quick guide to seven of the best.

Timber:
Timber is often overlooked because it is considered inappropriate for our climate, which is completely untrue! It's a perfect choice, and can be so versatile. Options vary, but hardwoods are best. Cedar when left untreated will turn a lovely silvery grey to blend in with the landscape. Larch can be charred or burned to give a striking black appearance, and is sealed with a special oil to preserve its finish. A great material that is perfectly at home inside and out.

Plaster render:
This is what we see everywhere, and is a simple mix of sand and cement that gives a wall it's weatherproofing. It's actually quite versatile, in that you can paint it any colour (or you can apply a colour to the render itself) and the finishes vary from silky smooth to rough to a heavier dashed finish. I have seen a lot of creativity with render in the last few years – it's a great staple.

Concrete:
This can be used not only for the structure of a house but also as an external finish material, and it can look and function amazingly well. Good-quality faced concrete can be almost silk-like to the touch, beautiful to look at, and give peak levels of performance in terms of durability and maintenance. So much more than a clunky structural material.

Stone:
Stone can come in different varieties and styles of installation, and it always makes an impact. It gives such solidity and weight to a building, and can be extremely decorative. It weathers well, it is maintenance-free and will last a lifetime.

Metal (zinc and copper):

These metals, which can be used for roof finishes as well, are naturally resistant to corrosion, are extremely durable and require almost zero maintenance. In addition, the flexibility, malleability and versatility of these metals combined with their pleasing appearance often mean they're suitable for intricate shapes and forms.

Fibre cement:

This is a composite material that comes in any number of colours and can be used to create interesting patterns and effects. It is durable and versatile, has a smooth finish, and can look like a large cladding tile.

Brick:

Brick is the king as far as I am concerned. Working with it will change you as an architect, as you really appreciate just how beautiful, versatile, functional and simple it really is, given the number of finishes and colours it is available in. There are also a whole host of different mortar joint designs as well as techniques in the laying of the brick to give patterns and effects that add yet another layer to its diversity.

It has played an important role in our built heritage, as it was used for much of the building stock in and around the terraced houses we see everywhere. It can look simultaneously traditional and contemporary and never dates – it has a timeless quality to it.

Design: Studio Red Architects; Image: Philip Lauterbach Photography

Design: ODKM Architects; Image: Barbara Egan

(Left) Design: Studio Red Architects; Image: Peter Grogan/Emagine; (Right) Design: ODKM Architects; Image: Declan O'Donnell

(Left) Design: NOJI Architects; Image: Alice Clancy Photography; (Right) Design: ODKM Architects; Image: Ned Kelly/Imageart Photography

Whatever your design looks like, the materials used should be sensitive to its context, and should embody what the design is trying to achieve. The design could call for a contrast in materials, maybe in order to make a statement. Or it could be about being sympathetic to an existing structure or shape or form. At the end of the day, it should be responsive.

I have been to countless homes where a quick extension was put on to give some much-needed additional space, but it was poorly considered, and in some cases badly built, and the end result is accepted as a mistake. In issues like this, budget and timeframes were usually tight so the extension was constructed as fast as possible with little thought to design. When budgets are tight, you need to spend *extra* time, thought and effort to ensure you are doing the right thing, and that it is done correctly to meet your needs long into the future. I've always found the dichotomy of this really quite frustrating because wasting hard-earned money is not nice for anyone, and it can be avoided. It's common sense, but the rule is: Do it once and do it right.

Creating beautiful, functional and dramatic rooms that connect with the outdoors, and bring a sense of joy to the home is what extending is all about.

WHERE TO EXTEND?

To the rear

Given the principles of house design in general (front door, back garden, bedrooms upstairs, kitchen at the back) most houses are able to add a single-storey extension to the rear. This also taps into the shift in modern living where we want bigger and more open kitchens as part of a generous open-plan area where everyone can eat, relax, watch television or do their homework.

Our desire for these spaces, combined with the fact that we can extend up to a certain size without planning permission (see page 234 for more on exempted developments) means this is the go-to for most people wanting to add value and space to their home.

Design: Plus Architecture; Image: Donal Murphy Photography

Extending to the rear usually means more privacy and better connected spaces to the garden. It also allows you to go for something in total contrast to the architecture of the rest of the house.

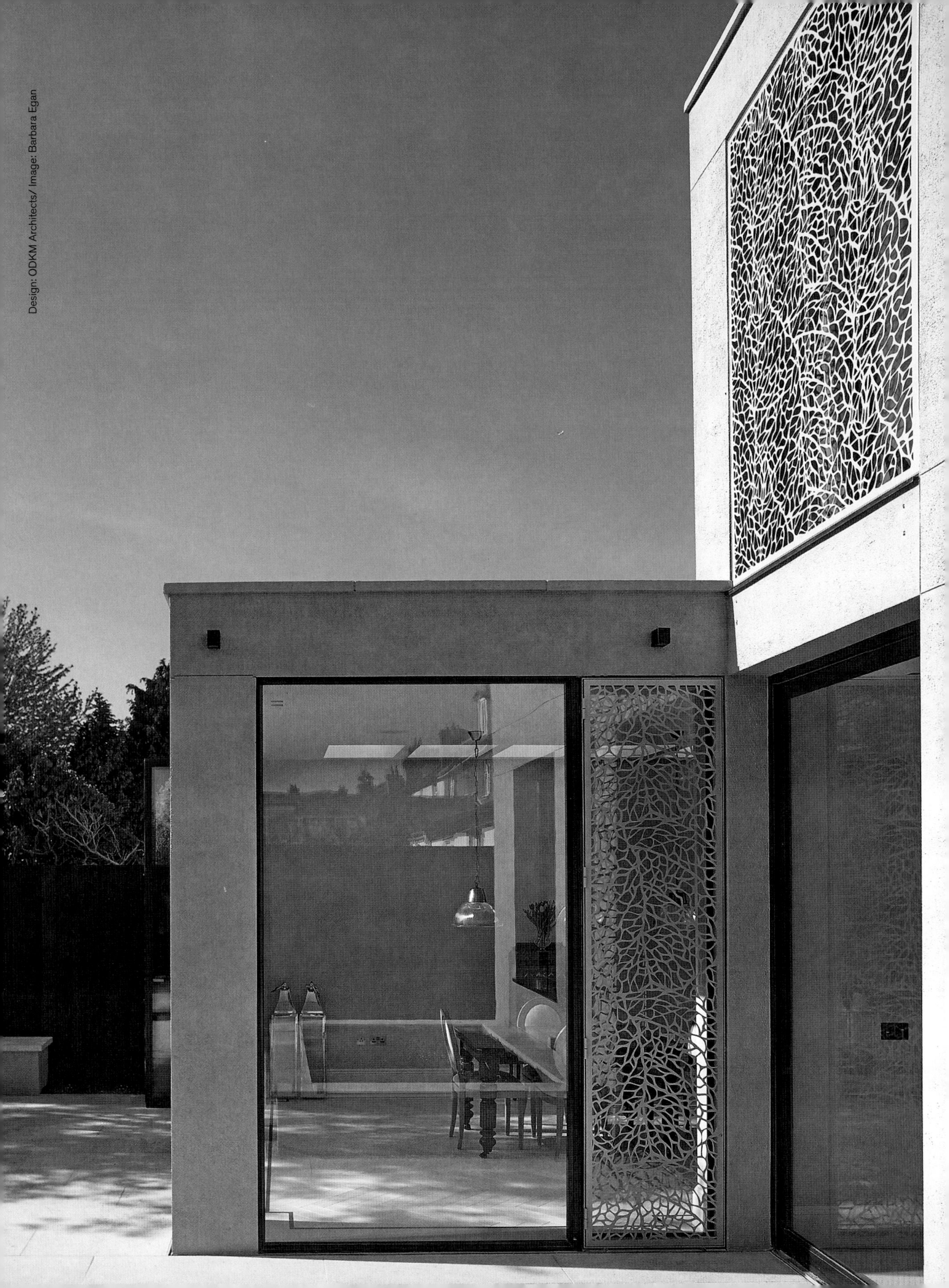

Design: ODKM Architects/ Image: Barbara Egan

To the front

Extending to the front is a pretty difficult thing to do, and has a whole host of constraints that means it's not done very often. Smaller front gardens, parking cars and just the configuration of most houses means that they don't lend themselves naturally to benefit from front extensions. A small porch is about as far as most people go.

Front porches can be a very useful extra room to the front of the house, especially if the current front door opens directly into the hallway. Anything over 2 square metres will require planning permission, but as always, changes to the front of your house should be sense checked with the local planning authorities.

Most houses share a common arrangement. Usually one half has the 'better' proportioned rooms, there's a hallway or spine that connects the various rooms and smaller ancillary support spaces – like bathrooms – off to one side or tucked away somewhere. This means that, when you extend, you really want to keep the 'best' side of the house, and look at changing the side that is less attractive. It's not always possible to do this but, generally speaking, the better characteristics of any house are the ones you want to maintain, and I always think good design does this and finds the answers it needs elsewhere.

To the side

Side extensions are quite popular because they often involve converting a garage, which makes it quite easy to add a second storey that can wrap around to the back of the house as well. These are great for adding a downstairs bedroom or den area, along with a proper bedroom upstairs in place of the small box room. This is adding real value to your home in terms of quality of space (bigger bedrooms) and also value in terms of what the home now has to offer.

Second storey

Adding a two-storey extension, either to the side or to the rear of an existing two-storey house, can add significant space and value to your home. Again, this is usually done to create an extra bedroom and, if so, it often becomes the master bedroom, as it will probably be the biggest bedroom in the house, so you should also consider adding a dressing room and en-suite. The issue is always in how the new rooms

Design: Studio Red Architects; Image: Philip Lauterbach Photography

can plug in to the existing staircase and back to the existing house. This is where the spine of the house, the stairs and the hallways, need to be in the right place to facilitate the link at upper level but it would be important to seek advice on this from a qualified architect as an extension done badly without proper planning could dramatically reduce the value, flow and functionality of your home.

Attic

If you have a good pitch on the existing roof of your house, and you need extra space for a bedroom, office or a hangout space, the answer could be to convert your attic. I love attic spaces because you can touch the angle of the roof plane, and they produce interesting shapes and are therefore interesting rooms to be in – very different from the usual box shape of other rooms in the house. They're also miles away from everyone else, so they're a bit of an oasis for both adults and kids. Added to that, the views can be great from that height so they can be great spaces if you get them right.

Attic conversions make a great small office to prevent paperwork and files cluttering up the dining room or spare bedroom, so if you need a dedicated work area it makes sense to have a separate room away from the shared spaces in the house. Kids grow, and so does the amount of stuff they need; one room may no longer be suitable for two or more siblings, so going into the attic can be a really cost-effective way of gaining an extra bedroom at a fraction of the cost of an extension. They can even double up as guest bedrooms when needed so if you have the space, they can be flexible spaces that become invaluable over time in lots of different ways.

You will need to check your head heights to see if it will be worthwhile converting as if you're already hitting your head up there it will never be a proper room – but it might not have to be. It could still work perfectly as a children's den; the point is, if you have some good space up there, make use of it.

There are some technical things to consider about attics – they can be complicated enough spaces because all the roof angles are sloping and crashing into one another so it's hard to tell if a staircase will work or not.

Below are some things you will need to consider if you are thinking of converting your attic.

Habitable room:

If you're converting your attic because you want it to be used as a bedroom (and when selling the house, you want to show it as an extra bedroom), then you need to make sure at least 50 per cent of your floor area has a head height above 2.4 metres. If it doesn't, the room will only ever be classed as storage. A dormer extension can increase the head height in areas to get you over that threshold, but this will need planning permission

Skylights:

You will want to include skylights in your conversion. You will need planning permission to put them on the front of the house, but to the rear is OK without planning permission.

Staircase:

As with any new staircase, it will need to conform with the current regulations, so it is always best to check with an architect or design professional to ensure the new works are in compliance.

Fire:

In a two-storey house, converting the attic is effectively adding a third storey, which means the house will now need to comply with fire regulations. This requires you to have a safe route of escape from the attic in the event of a fire in another room, as it is not acceptable to jump from a window or be rescued at that height. The impact of this is that the hallway must become fire protected from top to bottom, front door to attic. All doors on the hallway (from bedrooms) will need to be replaced by fire doors and they must have self-closing mechanisms fitted. If you have large sliding doors downstairs that you like to keep open all the time, these will also need to have self-closing mechanisms retro-fitted, so there is an impact throughout the house from top to bottom in deciding to convert the attic.

Floor:

The existing attic may be fine for the odd suitcase, but an engineer will need to specify the works required to make sure the new floor is structurally satisfactory for habitable use. This involves the insertion of steel sections or girders, which will also reduce the floor-to-ceiling height

Storage

You will still have lots of storage in the eaves, so always include multiple doors to gain access into these areas – don't worry, the Christmas tree will still have a place to call home. Christmas tree, suitcases, junk, golf clubs, junk, some boxes, more junk – our attics are filled with rubbish! Get everything out of there and have a good look at what you have and think about what you could do with the space.

COURTYARDS

Connecting a room or a series of rooms to an existing house is always a challenge, particularly in relation to light. Adding rooms to the back of a house will always pose questions about how to deal with the original spaces within the house, such as the addition of rooms may take away some of the natural light. Well, no surprise, nature (and history) has the answer.

Design: Greenstone Landscapes; Image: Barbara Egan

Courtyards have been used in architecture for as long as humans have been building houses, dating as far back as 6000 BC, and have been used for sleeping, cooking, playing, gardening and keeping animals. They have progressed and evolved through the years in tandem with human and house evolution, and modern courtyards in domestic architecture provide a light, airy, secure and private enclosed outdoor space. They also open the possibility of adding space without compromise to the existing rooms within a building. A conundrum I face every day when talking to clients about their houses.

Happily, a courtyard can be ultra-effective on even a very small scale. Architects often create such small courtyard spaces that introduce light, air and nature into houses that are being extended. You can't underestimate nature's role in this. Bringing vibrant green plant life into these spaces is a key factor in their success. If you can get a table and chair out there as well then all the better, but at the very least make sure it is full of life, as the lack of this compromises the courtyard entirely.

Design: Katie Jakkulla, Jakkulla Architecture & Design; Image: Barbara Egan

Design: Amanda Bone Architects; Image: Ros Kavanagh Photographer

PITFALLS

I'm often asked for top tips to prevent disaster before starting to build on site, or if extensively renovating your home. So I've included below the five biggest mistakes to avoid when taking on a project like this. I could probably add another few on here, but I think these are the bare minimum.

1. **Don't go to a builder first**

   If a builder has been recommended to you, then great, certainly talk to them, but, first and foremost, get an architect and make sure they are registered with the RIAI – this is the regulatory body in Ireland and will ensure that you are hiring a professional with the requisite skill to manage and advise on every aspect of your project from start to finish. This will save you time and money in the long run, and give you a home that is both functioning and well-designed. Your home is the biggest investment you will ever make so you have to make sure it's in good hands!

   Take time selecting the *right* architect for you – homes are so personal and emotional that the relationship you have with your architect will be crucial.

2. **Be honest and realistic about cost, time and quality**

   Have a good think about how much you can spend – and be realistic – for everything, and stick to your budget. What are your priorities? Is it to do something fast? Is it to add real quality and value to your home? There is no such thing as achieving something fast, cheap and of high quality – good design takes time, not only to get it right but also to look at alternatives to make sure what you are about to do is the right thing for you and your home, both now and in the years to come. When you move fast, you make mistakes.

   Whatever your project, always add about 5–10 per cent to your budget as a contingency sum for the unforeseen issues that may arise. This is fundamental to keeping your stress levels down!

3. **Be careful who you listen to**

   Everyone will have an opinion on the work you are about to carry out – from your colour choice, to layout design, materials, builders and style. This can cause you to become confused and unsure about what you really want and need, and can add to your stress levels. Doubt can creep in and I have seen clients who start to panic and make really bad choices.

   Design is a process, and this will distil what your design brief is – so trust this process and trust that the design you have settled on is the right one for *you*. Stay calm, keep on track – and trust your architect!

Design: Studio Red Architects; Image: Peter Grogan/Emagine

4. Fabric first – invest in the right things

Don't jump too far ahead and start picking out bathrooms and kitchens at the very start of your project. I know these are the beautiful things we are bombarded with in magazines every day, and can sometimes be the main reason for the project – but if your plan is to stay in a home for the next twenty-five years and you need serious upgrading work done, in terms of energy efficiency, insulation and windows, then these should be your priority. I know it's not sexy but it has to be done. This will add the real value and comfort to your home, and ensure it is in good shape going forward. Then you can be realistic about how much to spend on the kitchen in the overall context of the project, and not the other way around. (Refer back to points number 1 and 3!).

5. Sign a contract – and try to enjoy it

Don't be stressed! This is easier said than done, I know, but that is why investing the time in selecting and trusting your architect is so important. Sign a contract with your builder; a standard RIAI contract is more than sufficient, and it contains everything you will need to protect yourself throughout the building phase. It also protects the contractor, so it ensures everyone is fair and honest to the terms they signed up to.

The scope of work to be done is crucial, hence why the tender stage (see p. 231 'Working with an Architect') is so important, as it will state clearly what work is to be carried out and the builder's price for doing it – so if there is an extra, or you hit a problem, it is clear what is included and what is not. This is only fair for all concerned.

The architect will steer you through anything, so embrace good design, get involved with your architect and get passionate about the designs they're working on for you. You might think I sound crazy but changing your home really does have the power to change how you live for the better, and how to be more comfortable and happy in your home in the future. It's a brilliant and transformative process and you will never regret it, so try and have fun along the way!

Planning permission

If you are extending your house or undertaking significant refurbishment work, then you may need to apply to your local authority for planning permission, or if you live on a newer estate or within an apartment block you might also need to seek approval from the management company. Planning permission is something that seems to have developed a reputation for being notoriously difficult to obtain, or is so much hassle that it doesn't warrant following through with a particular design option. I am forever at a loss to understand this preconception. Good architecture is responsive to its environment, and is acutely aware of its context. Planning permission is nothing to be afraid of, providing you have a well-designed and responsive design.

This does not mean your design needs be traditional or conservative – it can actually be hugely radical, as long as there is merit in the design that the planners can recognise.

We have designed and built some contemporary and daring designs in the past few years and all of them sailed through the planning process – so it's not as scary as you may think.

I equate it to going into court with a solicitor. Some cases will be straightforward, some will be tricky, and some will have a few grey areas that will need professional judgement, and discussion with the judge. In this scenario, your architect is your barrister and will prepare the case for presentation and discussion – but ultimately, it's the judge's decision to make, so you need to think about what kind of architect will suit your project best.

Design: Amanda Bone Architects; Images: Ros Kavanagh Photographer

Working with an architect

A quick note on finding the right architect for you – all architects are different and offer varying degrees of specialities across a vast professional field. It is a good idea to meet with a few and interview them to see if their specialities match with your own passions for the project and what you want to achieve – just be prepared to be interviewed back. Design is a two-way process, which becomes even more intense if you're designing someone's home, so the relationship really has to work. It can be the beginning of a two- or three-year process in design and construction, through the inevitable ups and downs, so it's important to get the right fit for you and the needs of your project. As an example, a three-bed semi-detached house requiring a single-storey extension can take a full eighteen months from the first meeting, through the design stages to being finished on site, so it's a long process.

Your relationship with your architect will be tested, and trust is a huge factor in ensuring everything stays on track. As designs change, especially during construction, the architect is the only person who can see the bigger picture clearly. They will also know you well by the time construction begins, so will flag any honest or naive mistakes that you might make unknowingly.

I see this with clients all the time – they overthink so much during construction that they begin to make rash decisions – decisions that are totally against what they actually want, but they can't see it. Their eye is off the end game, they dig their heels in a bit and, before you know it, there's an impasse. People in creative industries often jokingly say to clients, 'Be careful, or I will give you exactly what you want.' It's a bit extreme, but you get the picture!

I can't speak on behalf of every architect, but sometimes when you think your architect is being difficult, they are actually working their hardest for you. Providing you choose well at the start, they will steer you through the good and the bad, and will keep *you* on track, for the building *you* want. It's OK to have differing opinions (in fact sometimes it's essential to peel into deeper layers of design), but the common goal is always to give the client the building they want and need. The architect never loses sight of this – so trust your architect.

Be involved in the process, ask questions, ask more questions. Give feedback. Engage. Don't be afraid! Behind every good project is a good client.

Exemptions

Some smaller projects don't require planning permission, and they're generally towards the rear of the house (so you can't really see them from the street level) and small in size, under 40 square metres. This relates to additional areas to the *original* footprint of the house – so if you have already converted your garage into a living room or an extra bedroom, then the size of this conversion must be subtracted from your 40 square metres. Roof heights are capped at 4 metres for pitched roofs, and 3 metres for all others, including flat roofs. There is an allowance of 12 square metres from the 40 metres that can be used at first-floor level, but I would advise seeking professional advice before embarking on this option as there are other planning criteria involved that will need the input of an architect.

There are certain thresholds relating to size or height to which, when exceeded, the exemptions will no longer apply so it is always better to check with the local planning authority.

Porches can change your life if you live in a small house. You can build a porch without planning permission, as long as it does not exceed 2 square metres in area and is more than 2 metres from any public road or footpath. Where the porch has a tiled or slated pitched roof, it must not exceed 4 metres in height, or 3 metres for any other roof type.

Non-exemptions

If you own a protected structure, or live in an architectural conservation area, then there will be limitations to what you can do with your house. In these cases, it is always better to ask an architect for advice as most exemptions will not apply.

WINDOWS

There are also rules about the required distances between windows in extensions, the facing boundary of the adjoining property and the use of the roof of the extension. Any windows proposed at ground-floor level as part of an extension should be not less than 1 metre from the boundary they face, and any windows proposed above ground level should be not less than 11 metres from the boundary they face. Also, if you have a flat-roof extension, this cannot be used as a balcony or a terrace.

Design: Carson & Crushell Architects; Image: Henrietta Williams

Don't be afraid of planning permission! It's actually quite straightforward, and the rigour involved in it will lead the project in the right way. Planners sometimes get a hard time, but they are there to protect the landscape and the urban context. They will react against anything that disregards basic planning principles, or has an adverse impact on the immediate and wider context of the building and any changes proposed – and this is a good thing. Good architecture responds to all of this context, and you will be surprised at what the authorities are open to.

Planning application

Engaging with planners early in the project is always beneficial. It opens up the dialogue and lets them know that there is potential work being planned for a given house. It can also flag up any serious issues with drainage or boundaries that are better to deal with early on rather than when the application goes in. The actual application itself is a series of drawings, maps, letters, forms and images that accurately convey the design intent in full to the planning authority. A legal notice will need to be printed in the newspaper, and local authorities will give a list of approved publications. Local newspapers will always cost much less than the nationals, and as these adverts can be quite word heavy, the costs can easily run to €400 so it is worth shopping around.

As well as this, a site notice needs to be displayed at the house/front gate and must be in place for five weeks. Always make sure it is erect and visible because failure to ensure this is displayed fully during this time can invalidate the application.

Design: ODKM Architects; Image: Ned Kelly/Imageart Photography

Timeframes

I always get asked this question about timeframes through planning, so below is a rough guide to the time involved after you submit your application.

- A five-week period for observations. This coincides with the length of time the site notice needs to be on show, and is the time period allowed for third parties to make an objection or observation on the application. They may have a concern over a certain issue, so they have a concise period of time in which to make their concerns official if they wish to do so.

- Three-week period for notification of the decision. This will also be circulated to those who lodged observations.

- Four-week period for the final notification, which gives time for any third parties to lodge an appeal if they wish to do so.

The planning process is just that – a process. There can be unforeseen requests from the authorities and, from time to time, depending on the project, they may ask for additional information in order to make their decision. Architects generally don't build this into their fee because it is simply not known from the start, so it would be unfair to do so, and bulk up their fee for work that may not be required. As I have said before, trust your architect.

When the decision comes through, all being well there will be a set of conditions marked out that clearly state any specific comments in relation to the project. The planning approval is valid for five years.

Be neighbourly

Most third parties who become embroiled in planning application disputes live near the house being renovated/extended, so it is basic common courtesy to speak with your neighbours if you are planning extensive work.

Building work can be noisy and disruptive, and your now-tranquil back garden can be turned into a building site over the weekend, so if you share boundaries and live with neighbours, it's always a good idea to call in and talk them through your plans. You can accommodate their concerns and feed them back into the design if needed, and this will help with relations going forward.

We always advise clients to do this before the planning application goes in and a site notice appears in the front garden. A good architect will be wary of the context and will take into consideration the neighbouring conditions when designing a tricky extension, for example – so hopefully they can see this if it is explained to them, so that they feel involved in the process. This will help greatly once the project starts, trust me.

BE YOURSELF

Many of us think of our home as a showpiece, something for someone else. While there is nothing wrong with a bit of house pride, the very essence of a home is personal. It's a sanctuary, a place to be yourself, a place to be happy.

We surround ourselves with everything we hold most dear, we welcome friends with open arms and when the day is done we settle down with our loved ones. At home, we are safe, we are at peace, we are happy.

I believe a key to that happiness lies in using design to make your home a better place for you. So no matter what your budget is, or what size project you are thinking of taking on, good design has the answer, and we should be focusing on this when redesigning or remodelling our homes. Whatever the problem, the rules are to keep things simple and listen to yourself and the house that you live in.

On a deeper level, there is a language and a connection between who we are and where we live. These spaces communicate who we are to the greater world, which is not just a one-way process – they also serve to remind us about who we are. We are different people at home – hidden away from the day to day, the outside world and all its troubles. There is a restfulness that comes from being home, from finally returning to the comfort of our true selves. This is why our homes are so important to all of us.

Design: Eimear Nic An Bhaird; Image: Barbara Egan

acknowledgements

Writing a book about home design made me think about my own family home growing up, and it reminded me that this is where lifelong memories are made. I was always warm, happy and safe – so I want to thank my parents, my brother and my two sisters for always being there for me.

I also have to thank a few people for helping me pull all this together. Firstly my editor, Ciara Doorley, for her patience in dealing with a first-time writer, and for her kind direction. I also need to thank Joanna Smyth for her relentless efforts in pulling all of the images and permissions from a wide range of sources together. This was a huge task, and fundamental to how this book looks, so thank you. Kathryn Meghen at the RIAI for her help with sourcing some of the images for the book, along with various architects and designer friends for their contributions and support. Ciaran and Barry in the office are a constant source of entertainment, encouragement and sound advice as we build a practice together, and are credited with bringing me back to Ireland – a move I will never regret. My siblings and all my little nieces and nephews who are always there when I need them, and help even when they don't know it.

Lastly to my ever-suffering partner Judith, who has to live with an architect. There must be a support group somewhere, Jude! Thank you x

Permissions Acknowledgements

The author and publisher would like to thank the following for permission to use inside photographs in *Rooms*:

Amanda Bone Architects and Ros Kavanagh Photographer: 30 (middle left), 88, 226–227, 230 (both images).

Carson & Crushell Architects: 48–49, 124 (image by Dariusz Cyparski), 211 (bottom), 235 (image by Henrietta Williams).

Darragh Lynch Architects and Donal Murphy Photography: 31 (middle), 68–69.

Dean Cooper & Company (www.deancooper.ie) and Infinity Media: 92–93, 139 (right), 158–159, 197 (both images), 202, 203.

Douglas Wallace Consultants: 200–201

De Siún Scullion Architects: 82 (right), 87 (Images by Paul Tierney Photography); 163 (Image by Philip Lauterbach Photography)

Dora Hurley and Barbara Egan: 150–151.

Dulux Paints Ireland: 9, 30–31 (colour chips), 45, 46, 50–51, 55 (all images), 56–57, 89, 97, 107, 119 (bottom), 123, 135 (bottom), 143 (top right), 154 (top right), 164, 240.

©Ebony and Co: viii, 20–21, 30(middle right), 35, 37, 39, 41–41,91, 102–103, 190–191.

Eimear Nic An Bhaird and Barbara Egan: 239.

© Getty Images: 30–31 & 146–147/Westend1, 43/Andrew MacDonald, 72/ Lived In Images, 79/moodboard, 137 (bottom left)/ CaialmageCLOSED, 137 (top)/180–181/183 (left)/199 (top)/Astronaut Images, 139 (left)/182/ Caiaimage/Tom Merton, 160–161/Halfdark, 166/ stocknroll, 170–171/OJO_Images, 174/ Perry Mastrovito, 179/Kim Mayer, 184/Rick Lew, 192/Fuse, 169 (left)/194/195/Hero Images, 169 (right)/carlofranco, 199 (bottom left)/Eric Hernandez, 205/Melissa Ross, 206–207/Daly and Newton, 222/Peter Mukherjee.

Greenstone Landscapes and Barbara Egan: 224.

©iStock/archideaphoto: 84–85.

Kingston Lafferty Design and Donal Murphy Photography: 13, 32, 70, 82 (left), 83, 94, 98–99, 109 (bottom), 119 (top), 121, 127 (left), 143 (bottom), 152–153.

Martins Camisuli Architects and Jake Fitzjones Photography: 101, 176.

Maxime Laroussi/Urban Agency and Barbara Egan: 63, 116, 167 (both images).

Katie Jakkulla, Jakkulla Architecture & Design and Barbara Egan: 199 (bottom right), 225.

NOJI Architects and Alice Clancy Photography: 132 (bottom right), 143 (top left), 154 (bottom right), 157, 208, 211 (top), 215 (left).

ODKM Architects: vi, 19, 27, 28, 132, 214 (top), 218–219 (Images: Barbara Egan); 12, 31, 214 (bottom right) (Image: Declan O'Donnell); 16, 114–115 (Image: Sasfi Hope Ross); 100, 154 (left) (Image: Rory Corrigan Photography); 215 (right), 236 (Image: Ned Kelly/Imageart Photography)

Plotscape and durstonphoto.com: 232–233.

Plus Architecture and Donal Murphy Photography: 75, 104, 110, 128, 216, 217. (Rainey Residence, Sandymount, Dublin 4 – completed 2015. Design by: Plus Architecture. Architects: Lucy Rainey & Des Twomey)

Porter & Jones Kitchen: ii, 6, 127 (right), 140–141.

ODKM Architects and Porter & Jones Kitchen: 22 (both images), 30 (bottom left), 130–131, 138.

© Shutterstock.com: 25/ Pablo Scapinachis, 30–31(background)/ The_Pixel, 30 (top right)/ Everything, 30(top left)/Venus Angel, 31 (pen)/iunewind, 31/macknimal, 53 (bottom middle)/ topnatthapon, 53 (bottom right)/Margo Harrison, 53 (bottom left)/145 (top) Jodie Johnson, 53 (top)/bikeriderlondon, 58/Mr. jub, 59/scenery2, 61/ Photographee.eu, 105/223/ adpePhoto, 106/137 (bottom right)/196 (right)/photobank.ch, 109 (top)/Gorin, 117 (both images)/ MR INTERIOR, 129/karamysh, 132 (bottom right)/134/173 (bottom)/193/ ariadna de raadt, 135 (top)/nomadFra, 145 (bottom)/jokerpro, 178 (right)/Sylvie Bouchard, 178 (left)/Kuznetsov Alexey, 183 (right)/ Wuttichok Panichiwarapun, 196 (left)/Worldwide.

Studio Red Architects: 39, 76, 213, 221 (Images by Philip Lauterbach Photography); 64–65, 175, 188, 214 (bottom left), 229 (Images by Peter Grogan/Emagine).

Think Contemporary and Barbara Egan: 186.

Tilestyle and Dúlra Photography: 59, 173 (top).

Wesley O'Brien Design and Barbara Egan: 81.

bibliography / useful websites

Below is a list of useful websites that are a great source of information, and useful pointers in the right direction.

Twitter @decodonn
Instagram DECODONNELL

ODKM Architects

My second home. This is where I work.
www.odkmarchitects.com

RIAI

Royal Institute of Architects in Ireland – your one-stop shop for everything you need to know about architecture, and the value you get from working with an architect.
www.riai.ie

ARCHITECTURE IRELAND

The journal of the RIAI – everything you need to know about Irish architecture.
www.architectureireland.ie

SEAI

Sustainable Energy Authority of Ireland – tips and guidance on improving energy efficiency in your home, saving money and information on grants available for sustainable home renovations.
www.seai.ie

HOUZZ

Image sourcing and design ideas – essential visual reference and tips for any home improvement.
www.houzz.co.uk

PINTEREST

More image sourcing and design ideas, similar to Houzz.

www.pinterest.com

DEZEEN

One of my favourite online design blogs.

www.dezeen.com/

LOCAL PLANNING AUTHORITIES

Useful portal link from which to find your local planning authority, and information on Building Control Regulations throughout Ireland.

www.environ.ie

IRISH ARCHITECTURE FOUNDATION

An introduction to the cultural significance of architecture in Ireland.

www.architecturefoundation.ie

SELF-BUILD

For all those seeking to self-build their project, this is an essential resource.

www.selfbuild.ie

ARCHISEEK

Great for keeping up to date with architecture in Ireland, old and new.

www.archiseek.com

DULUX PAINTS IRELAND

Great website for colour choice and advice when doing up your home, and still the best hardwearing quality paint around. They have an amazing visualiser app that everyone should know about!

www.dulux.ie

Notes

Notes